The history and description of the Isle of Man: viz its antiquity, history, laws, customs, Likewise many comical and entertaining stories of the pranks play'd by faries, from original papers and personal knowledge

George Waldron

The history and description of the Isle of Man: viz. its antiquity, history, laws, customs, ...
Likewise many comical and entertaining stories of the pranks play'd by faries, &c. The whole
carefully collected from original papers and personal knowledge, during near twenty years
residence there.
Waldron, George
ESTCID: N001423
Reproduction from Huntington Library
Anonymous. By George Waldron.
Dublin : printed for E. Rider, and J. Torbuck, [1742?].
95,[1]p.,plate ; 12°

Gale ECCO Print Editions

Relive history with *Eighteenth Century Collections Online*, now available in print for the independent historian and collector. This series includes the most significant English-language and foreign-language works printed in Great Britain during the eighteenth century, and is organized in seven different subject areas including literature and language; medicine, science, and technology; and religion and philosophy. The collection also includes thousands of important works from the Americas.

The eighteenth century has been called "The Age of Enlightenment." It was a period of rapid advance in print culture and publishing, in world exploration, and in the rapid growth of science and technology – all of which had a profound impact on the political and cultural landscape. At the end of the century the American Revolution, French Revolution and Industrial Revolution, perhaps three of the most significant events in modern history, set in motion developments that eventually dominated world political, economic, and social life.

In a groundbreaking effort, Gale initiated a revolution of its own: digitization of epic proportions to preserve these invaluable works in the largest online archive of its kind. Contributions from major world libraries constitute over 175,000 original printed works. Scanned images of the actual pages, rather than transcriptions, recreate the works *as they first appeared.*

Now for the first time, these high-quality digital scans of original works are available via print-on-demand, making them readily accessible to libraries, students, independent scholars, and readers of all ages.

For our initial release we have created seven robust collections to form one the world's most comprehensive catalogs of 18th century works.

Initial Gale ECCO Print Editions collections include:

History and Geography
Rich in titles on English life and social history, this collection spans the world as it was known to eighteenth-century historians and explorers. Titles include a wealth of travel accounts and diaries, histories of nations from throughout the world, and maps and charts of a world that was still being discovered. Students of the War of American Independence will find fascinating accounts from the British side of conflict.

Social Science

Delve into what it was like to live during the eighteenth century by reading the first-hand accounts of everyday people, including city dwellers and farmers, businessmen and bankers, artisans and merchants, artists and their patrons, politicians and their constituents. Original texts make the American, French, and Industrial revolutions vividly contemporary.

Medicine, Science and Technology

Medical theory and practice of the 1700s developed rapidly, as is evidenced by the extensive collection, which includes descriptions of diseases, their conditions, and treatments. Books on science and technology, agriculture, military technology, natural philosophy, even cookbooks, are all contained here.

Literature and Language

Western literary study flows out of eighteenth-century works by Alexander Pope, Daniel Defoe, Henry Fielding, Frances Burney, Denis Diderot, Johann Gottfried Herder, Johann Wolfgang von Goethe, and others. Experience the birth of the modern novel, or compare the development of language using dictionaries and grammar discourses.

Religion and Philosophy

The Age of Enlightenment profoundly enriched religious and philosophical understanding and continues to influence present-day thinking. Works collected here include masterpieces by David Hume, Immanuel Kant, and Jean-Jacques Rousseau, as well as religious sermons and moral debates on the issues of the day, such as the slave trade. The Age of Reason saw conflict between Protestantism and Catholicism transformed into one between faith and logic -- a debate that continues in the twenty-first century.

Law and Reference

This collection reveals the history of English common law and Empire law in a vastly changing world of British expansion. Dominating the legal field is the *Commentaries of the Law of England* by Sir William Blackstone, which first appeared in 1765. Reference works such as almanacs and catalogues continue to educate us by revealing the day-to-day workings of society.

Fine Arts

The eighteenth-century fascination with Greek and Roman antiquity followed the systematic excavation of the ruins at Pompeii and Herculaneum in southern Italy; and after 1750 a neoclassical style dominated all artistic fields. The titles here trace developments in mostly English-language works on painting, sculpture, architecture, music, theater, and other disciplines. Instructional works on musical instruments, catalogs of art objects, comic operas, and more are also included.

The BiblioLife Network

This project was made possible in part by the BiblioLife Network (BLN), a project aimed at addressing some of the huge challenges facing book preservationists around the world. The BLN includes libraries, library networks, archives, subject matter experts, online communities and library service providers. We believe every book ever published should be available as a high-quality print reproduction; printed on-demand anywhere in the world. This insures the ongoing accessibility of the content and helps generate sustainable revenue for the libraries and organizations that work to preserve these important materials.

The following book is in the "public domain" and represents an authentic reproduction of the text as printed by the original publisher. While we have attempted to accurately maintain the integrity of the original work, there are sometimes problems with the original work or the micro-film from which the books were digitized. This can result in minor errors in reproduction. Possible imperfections include missing and blurred pages, poor pictures, markings and other reproduction issues beyond our control. Because this work is culturally important, we have made it available as part of our commitment to protecting, preserving, and promoting the world's literature.

GUIDE TO FOLD-OUTS MAPS and OVERSIZED IMAGES

The book you are reading was digitized from microfilm captured over the past thirty to forty years. Years after the creation of the original microfilm, the book was converted to digital files and made available in an online database.

In an online database, page images do not need to conform to the size restrictions found in a printed book. When converting these images back into a printed bound book, the page sizes are standardized in ways that maintain the detail of the original. For large images, such as fold-out maps, the original page image is split into two or more pages

Guidelines used to determine how to split the page image follows:

• Some images are split vertically; large images require vertical and horizontal splits.
• For horizontal splits, the content is split left to right.
• For vertical splits, the content is split from top to bottom.
• For both vertical and horizontal splits, the image is processed from top left to bottom right.

Behold bright Virtues Glorious Emblem plac't
Beneath a Crown with beaming Stars Enchac't,
Virtue like Palms does under preßure rise,
And Phenix like true Virtue never dies.

THE
HISTORY
AND
DESCRIPTION
OF THE
ISLE of MAN:
VIZ.

Its Antiquity, History, Laws, Customs, Religion and Manners of its Inhabitants, its Animals, Minerals; Curious and Authentick Relations of APPARITIONS of GIANTS that have lived under the Castle Time immemorial.

Likewise many Comical and Entertaining Stories of the Pranks play'd by FARIES, &c.

The Whole carefully collected from Original Papers and Personal Knowledge, during near Twenty Years Residence there.

DUBLIN:

Printed for E. RIDER in *George's-Lane*, and J. TORBUCK at the *Bear* in *Skinner-Row*.

A
DESCRIPTION
OF THE
ISLE of MAN.

BETWEEN *Great Britain* and *Ireland* there is stretched out a considerable Island from North to South, about Thirty *Italian* Miles in Length; but where wideft, not above Fifteen in Breadth. The feveral ancient Writers have given it feveral Names: by *Cæfar* 'tis called *Mona*, by *Ptolemy*, *Monœda*, by *Pliny*, *Monabia*; and the fame Variety appears in fuch of our modern Authors, as make mention of it. It was firft inhabited by the *Britons*, then by the *Scots*, or *Picts*, and afterwards by the *Norwegians*, who had it in their Poffeffion a long Time: it fince paffed thro' a ftrange Diverfity of Revolutions, and at length, fell into the Hands of the *Englifh*, about the latter End of *Edward* the Firft, and remains to this Day under their Jurifdiction. It has had feveral Lords; fuch generally as had the greateft Intereft in our Princes: till the Grant thereof, together with the Patronage of the Bifhoprick, was made to Sir *John Stanley*, and his Heirs, by King *Henry* the Fourth; in which Family it is ftill continued.

Thus far the Account given by Mr. *Moll* in his

Compleat

Compleat Geographer may be depended on, but he is guilty of a grofs Miftake, in faying the Soil is extremely fruitful, and produces Wheat, Rye, and Barley, in fuch Plenty, that it not only furnifhes the Inhabitants, but likewife allows great Quantities to be exported. Whereas it is notorioufly known, that the little Wheat they have, is fo bad, that thofe who eat Bread made of it, have the Corn from *England* or *Ireland.* As for Rye, I never faw any there; Barley for the moft part they have enough of, to make Mault for themfelves, but never to fend abroad. Oats is their chief Produce, of which they make Bread, as alfo of Potatoes ; the Land affording fuch Abundance that Fields of them are almoft as common as Grafs.

As to the Seafons, three Parts of the Year is Winter, and the vaft Quantity of Snow and Rain, that are almoft continualy falling, fwells the Rivers to that Degree, that they frequently overflow the Lands, and do much Damage ; great Numbers of fmall Cattle, fuch as Sheep, Goats, and Hogs, being loft in them. Notwithftanding this, the Air is very wholefome, the Plague, nor any other contagious Diftemper having never been known there, and the People generally live to a very great Age.

The Black Cattle of this Ifland are excellently good, but fmall, as alfo their Sheep : it abounds in Hogs and Goats, Kid being as commonly eat there as Lamb in *England.* They have great Store of Poultry of all Sorts, except Turkies, which being ha   to rear, are not to be found but in particular Families. The near Neighbourhood of the Sea, and the Number of Rivers, afford very fine Fifh of all Kind, but efpecially Salmon and Cod : tho' Herrings are the chief Food of the poor People,

which

which are falted up in the Seafon to laft for the whole Year.

The Ifland being very rocky, the Buildings are moftly Stone, I mean thofe which are inhabited by the Gentry ; as for the others, they are no more than Cabins built of Sods, and covered with the fame, except a few belonging to the better Sort of Farmers, which are thatched with Straw : but in the midft of the utmoft Irregularity, they have two Conveniences, which fometimes the beft ordered Houfes cannot boaft of, the fineft Brooks in the World running continually near them, and Turf, which makes a very fweet Firing, at their very Doors. Their Towns are fix in Number, and called, 1. *Caftle-Town*, or *Ruffin*. 2. *Duglas*. 3. *Peel*, or *Pile*. 4. *Ramfay*. 5. *Ballafalli*. 6. *Macguires*, or *New-Town*.

Of thefe I fhall give a particular Defcription, having fpent a great deal of Time in examining feveral Curiofities and Antiquities which I believe no Author has yet ever treated on, but are very worthy of Obfervation. And firft of *Caftle-Town*.

It is the Metropolis of the Ifland, and the Place where moft of the Perfons of any Note chufe to have their Refidence, becaufe the Governor keeps his Court in it; the Caftle is a fine ancient Building, and has been honoured with the Prefence of feveral of the Lords of *Man*. The Courts of Judicature are alfo kept here, and what Records of the Ifland are yet remaining : but the greateft Part of them, in troublefome Times, were carried away by the *Norwegians*, and depofited among the Archives of the Bifhops of *Drunton* in *Norway*, where they ftill remain ; tho' a few Years fince, Mr. *Stephenfon*, an eminent, worthy, and learned Merchant of

A 3 — *Dublin*,

Dublin, offered the then Bishop of *Drunton* a considerable Sum of Money for the Purchase of them, designing to restore, and present them to the Island, but the Bishop of *Drunton* would not part with them on any Terms.

The Abridger of *Camden*'s *Britannia* makes mention of a little Isle within this Town, where Pope *Gregory* the Fourth erected an Episcopal See, but at present, there is no such Place to be found: nor is it probable it can have been swallowed up by the Sea, there being no low Grounds, but a high mountainous Shore all along that Part of the Island. He farther says, that among the *Hebrides*, generally reckoned Forty-four in Number, was the Isle of *Jona*, lying between *Ila* and *Scotland*, and called by *Bede*, *Hy* or *Hu*; and that, there was a Bishop's See erected in *Sodore*, a small Village, from which all the Islanders took the Name of *Sodorenses*, being all contained in his Diocess. But nothing is more certain, than that this Opinion is erroneous, for the Bishops of *Man*, do not take their Title of *Sodor* from the Island so called, but from the Church at *Peel*, called *Ecclesia Sodorensis*, dedicated to our Saviour. This is not only maintained by Archbishop *Spotswood*, and the most judicious Antiquaries, and Historians, but by the Tradition of the Natives themselves: Nor do I see any Reason to believe the Bishops of *Man* ever had any Jurisdiction over the *Hebrides*, because, were it so, some Accounts would have been handed down to Posterity, by what Means they had lost it: and as there is nothing but the Name of *Sodor* to countenance that Opinion, the Objection against it may easily be answered by what I have said.

The great Officers of the Island are first the *Governor*,

Governor, who, under the *Lord of Man*, has the entire Command of it; secondly, the two *Deempsters*, who are the Judges in Matters Civil and Criminal; thirdly, the *Comptroller*, who calls the Receiver-General to an Account; and fourthly, the *Receiver-General*, in whose Hands, all the inferior Collectors deposite the Rents due to the Lord.

Just at the Enterance of the Castle is a great Stone Chair for the *Governor*, and two lesser for the *Deempsters*. Here they try all Causes, except Ecclesiastick, which are entirely under the Decision of the *Bishop*; when you are past this little Court, you enter into a long winding Passage between two high Walls, not much unlike what is described of *Rosamond's* Labyrinth at *Woodstock*; in case of an Attack, Ten Thousand Men might be destroyed by a very few, in attempting to enter. The Extremity of it brings you to a Room where the *Keys* sit; they are Twenty-four in Number, they call them the Parliament; but in my Opinion, they more resemble our Juries in *England*; because the Business of their Meeting is to adjust Differences between the Common People, and are locked in till they have given their Verdict. They may be said in this Sense indeed, to be supreme Judges, because from them there is no Appeal but to the *Lord* himself.

A little farther, is an Apartment which has never been opened in the Memory of Man; the Persons belonging to the Castle, are very cautious in giving any Reason for it, but the Natives, who are excessively superstitious, assign this; That there is something of Inchantment in it. They tell you, that the Castle was at first inhabited by *Fairies*, and afterwards by *Giants*, who continued in the

Possession

Poffeffion of it till the Days of *Merlin*, who by the
Force of Magic diflodg'd the greateft Part of them,
and bound the reft in Spells, which they believe will
be indiffoluble to the End of the World : For Proof
of this, they tell you a very odd Story : They fay
there are a great Number of fine Apartments under-ground, exceeding in Magnificence any of the
upper Rooms; feveral Men of more than ordinary
Courage, have in former Times ventured down to
explore the Secrets of this fubterraneous Dwelling-
Place, but none of them ever returned to give an
Account of what they faw; it was therefore judged
convenient that all the Paffes to it fhould be kept
continually fhut, that no more might fufter by their
Temerity. But about fome Fifty or Fifty-five
Years fince, a Perfon who had an uncommon Boldnefs and Refolution, never left folliciting Permiffion of thofe who had the Power to grant it, to
vifit thofe dark Abodes: in fine, he obtained his
Requeft, went down, and returned by the Help
of a Clue of Packthread, which he took with him,
which no Man before himfelf had ever done ; and
brought this amazing Difcovery, *viz* That after
having paffed thro' a great Number of Vaults, he
came into a long narrow Place, which the farther he
penetrated, he perceived he went more and more
on a Defcent, till having travelled as near as he
could guefs, for the fpace of a Mile, he began to
fee a little Gleam of Light, which, tho' it feem'd
to come from a vaft Diftance, yet was the moft delightful Sight he had ever beheld in his Life. Having at length come to the End of that Lane of
Darknefs, he perceived a very large and magnificent Houfe, illuminated with a great many Candles,
whence proceeded the Light juft now mention'd :

having

having, before he begun this Expedition, well for-tified himself with Brandy, he had Courage enough to knock at the Door, which a Servant, at the third Knock, having open'd, ask'd him what he wanted. I would go as far as I can, reply'd our Adventurer; be so kind therefore to direct me how to accomplish my Design, for I see no Passage but that dark Cavern thro' which I came. The Servant told him, he must go thro' that House, and accordingly led him thro' a long Entry, and out at a Back-Door. He then walked a considerable Way, and at last beheld another House, more magnificent than the first; and the Windows being all open, discovered innumerable Lamps burning in every Room. Here he designed also to knock, but had the Curiosity to step on a little Bank which commanded a low Parlour; on looking in, he beheld a vast Table in the Middle of the Room of Black Marble, and on it, extended at full Length, a Man, or rather Monster; for by his Account, he could not be less than 14 Feet long, and 10 or 11 round the Body. This prodigious Fabrick lay as if sleeping, with his Head on a Book, and a Sword by him, of a Size answerable to the Hand which 'tis supposed made Use of it. This Sight was more terrifying to the Tra-veller, than all the dark and dreary Mansions he had passed thro' in his Arrival to it: he resolved therefore not to attempt Enterance into a Place in-habited by Persons of that unequal Stature, and made the best of his Way back to the other House, where the same Servant re-conducted, and inform-ed him, that if he had knocked at the second Door, he would have seen Company enough, but never could have returned. On which he desired to

know

know what Place it was, and by whom poffeffed;
but the other reply'd, that thefe Things were not
to be revealed. He then took Leave, and by the
fame dark Paffage got into the Vaults, and foon
after, once more afcended to the Light of the Sun.

Ridiculous as this Narrative appears, whoever
feems to disbelieve it, is looked on as a Perfon of a
weak Faith: but tho' this might be fufficient to
prove their Superftition, I cannot forbear making
mention of another Tradition they have, and of a
much longer ftanding I have already taken Notice
that their moft ancient Records were taken away
in a *Norwegian* Conqueft, which renders it impoffible to be certain how long the Ifland has been
found out, or by whom: to make up this Deficiency, they tell you this History of it.

Some Hundred Years, fay they, before the Coming of our Saviour, the Ifle of *Man* was inhabited by a certain Species call'd *Fairies*, and that every
Thing was carried on in a Kind of fupernatural Manner; that a blue Mift hanging continually over the
Land, prevented the Ships that paffed by, from having
any Sufpicion there was an Ifland This Mift, con-
trary to Nature, was preferved by keeping a perpetual Fire, which happening once to be extinguifhed,
the Shore difcovered itfelf to fome Fifhermen who
were then in a Boat on their Vocation, and by them
Notice was given to the People of fome Country (but
what, they do not pretend to determine) who fent
Ships in order to make a further Difcovery: That on
their landing, they had a fierce Encounter with the
little People, and having got the better over them,
poffefs'd themfelves of Caftle *Ruffin*, and by degrees,
as they received Reinforcements, of the whole
Ifland. Thefe new Conquerors maintained their
Ground

Ground some time, but were at length beaten out by a Race of *Giants*, who were not extirpated, as said before, till the Reign of Prince *Arthur*, by *Merlin*, the famous *British* Enchanter. They pretend also, that this Island afterward became an Asylum to all the distress'd Princes and Great Men in *Europe*, and that those uncommon Fortifications made about *Peel-Castle* were added for their better Security: but of this, I shall treat more copiously when I come to the Description of that Place.

The Tradition of what happened on suffering the domestic Fire to be extinct, remains in such Credit with them, that not a Family in the whole Island, to this Day, of the Natives, but keeps a small Quantity continually burning, no one daring to depend on his Neighbour's Vigilance in a Thing which he imagines is of so much consequence: every one confidently believing, that if it should ever happen that no Fire were to be found throughout, most terrible Revolutions and Mischiefs would immediately ensue.

The Castle, as also the two Walls which encompass it, and are broad enough for three Persons to walk a-breast on, are all of Free-stone, which is the only Building in the Island of that sort With-in the Walls is a small Tower adjoining to the Castle, where formerly State-Prisoners were kept, but serves now as a Store-house for the *Lord of Man's* Wines; it has a Moat round it, and Draw-bridge, and is a very strong Place. On the other side of the Castle, is the Governor's House, which is very commodious and specious. Here is also a fine Chapel where Divine Service is celebrated Morning and Afternoon, and several Offices belonging the Court of Chancery.

In

In this Town are the moſt regular Buildings in general of the whole Iſland, and within a ſhort Mile of it is *Derby-Haven,* which is by much the beſt Harbour they can boaſt of, and has a very ſtrong Fort in the Mouth of it.

Duglas, ſo called from the two Rivers running into that Harbour, and call'd the Black and the Grey Waters, muſt fall next under our Conſideration, as being the Town of the moſt Trade; and tho' theBuildings are very indifferent, and the near Neighbourhood of the Sea, which ſometimes runs mountain high, and in tempeſtuous Weather, threatens the Inhabitants with an Inundation; yet is full of very rich and eminent Dealers. The Reaſon of which is plain; the Harbour of it being the moſt frequented of any in the Iſland, by *Dutch, Iriſh,* and *Eaſt-India* Veſſels, there is the utmoſt Opportunity, that can be wiſhed, for carrying on the Smugling Trade. So much, it muſt be confeſs'd, do ſome Men prefer theirGain to their Safety, that they will venture it any where, but in this Place there is little Danger in infringing on the Rights of the Crown. And hear I muſt inform my Reader, that tho' his moſt Excellent Majeſty of *Great Britain* is Maſter of the Seas, yet the *Lord of Man* has the Juriſdiction of ſo much round the Iſland, that a Maſter of a Ship has no more to do than to watch his Opportunity of coming within the Piles, and he is ſecure from any Danger from the King's Officers. I myſelf had once Notice of a ſtately Pirate that was ſteering her Courſe into this Harbour, and would have boarded her before ſhe got within the Piles, but for want of being able to get ſufficient Help, could not execute my Deſign. Her Cargo was Indico, Maſtic, Raſins

Raiſins of the Sun, and other very rich Goods, which I had the Mortification to ſee ſold to the Traders of *Duglas* without the leaſt Duty paid to his Majeſty. The ſame Ship was taken afterwards near the Coaſt, by the Information I ſent of it to the Commiſſioners of the Cuſtoms.

Peel, or *Pile-Town,* is ſo called from its Garriſon and Caſtle; tho' in effect the Caſtle cannot properly be ſaid to be in theTown, anArm of theSea running between them, which in high Tides would be deep enough to bear a Ship of 40 or 50 Tun, tho' ſometimes quite drained of ſalt Water; but when it is ſupply'd with freſh by a River which runs from *Kirk Jarmyn* Mountains, and empties itſelf in the Sea. This Caſtle for its Situation, Antiquity, Strength and Beauty, might juſtly come in for one of the Wonders of the World. Art and Nature ſeem to have vied with each other in the Model, nor ought the moſt minute Particular to eſcape Obſervation.

As to its Situation, it is built upon the Top of a huge Rock, which rears itſelf a ſtupendous Height above the Sea, with which, as I ſaid before, it is ſurrounded. And alſo by natural Fortifications of other leſſer Rocks, which renders it unacceſſible but by paſſing that little Arm of the Sea which divides it from the Town; this you may do in a ſmall Boat: and the Natives, tucking up their Cloaths under their Arms, and plucking off their Shoes and Stockings, frequently wade it in low Tides. When you arrive at the Foot of the Rock, you aſcend about 60 Steps, which are cut out of to the firſt Wall, which is immenſely thick and high, and built of a very durable and bright Stone, tho' not of the ſame ſort with that of Caſtle *Ruſſin*

B in

in *Caſtle-Town*; and has on it four little Houſes or Watch-Towers, which overlook the Sea. The Gates are Wood, but moſt curiouſly arched, carved, and adorned with Pilaſters. Having paſſed the firſt, you have other Stairs of near half the Number with the former, to mount before you come at the ſecond Wall, which, as well as the other, is full of Port-holes for Cannon, which are planted on Stone Croſſes on a third Wall.

Being entered, you find yourſelf in a wide Plain, in the midſt of which ſtands the Caſtle, encompaſſed by four Churches, three of which, Time has ſo much decay'd, that there is little remaining beſides the Walls, and ſome few Tombs, which ſeem to have been erected with ſo much Care, as to perpetuate the Memory of thoſe buried in them, till the final Diſſolution of all Things. The fourth is kept a little better in Repair, but not ſo much for its own ſake, tho' it has been the moſt magnificent of them all, as for a Chapel within it, which is appropriated to the Uſe of the Biſhop, and has under it a Priſon, or rather Dungeon, for thoſe Offenders who are ſo miſerable as to incur the ſpiritual Cenſure; this is certainly one of the moſt dreadful Places that Imagination can form, the Sea runs under it thro' the Hollows of the Rock with ſuch a continual Roar, that you would think it were every moment breaking in upon you, and over it are the Vaults for burying the Dead. The Stairs deſcending to this Place of Terrors, are not above 30, but ſo ſteep and narrow, that they are very difficult to go down, a Child of eight or nine Years old not being able to paſs them but ſideways. Within it are 13 Pillars, on which the whole Chapel is ſupported: They have a ſuperſtition that

what

whatſoever Stranger goes to ſee this Cavern out of
Curioſity, and omits to count the Pillars, ſhall do
ſomething to occaſion being confined there.

There are Places for Penance alſo under all the o-
ther Churches, containing ſeveral very dark and horrid Cells ; ſome have nothing in them either to ſit or
lie down on, others a ſmall Piece of Brickwork ; ſome
are lower and more dark than others, but all of them,
in my Opinion, dreadful enough for almoſt any Crime
Humanity is capable of being guilty of, tho' 'tis ſuppoſed they were built with different Degrees of Horror, that the Puniſhment might be proportionate to
the Faults of thoſe Wretches who were to be confined
in them. Theſe have never been made uſe of, ſince the
Times of *Popery* but that under the Biſhop's Chapel
is the common, and only Priſon for all Offences in the
Spiritual Court, and to *that* the Delinquents are
ſentenced. But the Soldiers of the Garriſon per-
mit them to ſuffer their Confinement in the Caſtle,
it being morally impoſſible for the ſtrongeſt Con-
ſtitution to ſuſtain the Damps and Noiſomneſs of
the Cavern even for a few Hours, much leſs for
Months and Years, as is the Puniſhment ſometimes allotted. But I ſhall ſpeak hereafter more
fully of the Severity of the Eccleſiaſtical Juriſdiction.

'Tis certain that here have been very great Ar-
chitects in this Iſland ; for the noble Monuments
in this Church, which is kept in Repair, and indeed in the Ruins of the others alſo, ſhew the
Builders to be Maſters of all the Orders in that Art,
tho' the great Numbers of *Doric* Pillars prove them
to be chiefly Admirers of that.

Nor are the Epitaphs and Inſcriptions on the
Tomb-Stones leſs worthy of Remark: the various
Languages in which they are engraved, teſtify by

what

what a Diversity of Nations this little Spot of Earth has been possess'd. Tho' Time has defaced too many of the Letters to render the Remainder intelligible, yet you may easily perceive Fragments of the *Hebrew, Greek, Latin, Arabian, Saxon, Scotch,* and *Irish* Characters: some Dates yet visible, declare they were written before the Coming of *Christ*; and indeed if one considers the Walls, the Thickness of them, and the Durableness of the Stone of which they are composed, one must be sensible that a great Number of Centuries must pass before such strong Workmanship could be reduced to the Condition it now is. These Churches, therefore, were doubtless once the Temples of *Pagan* Deities, tho' since consecrated to the Worship of the true Divinity; and what confirms me more strongly in this Conjecture, is, that there is still a Part of one remaining, where stands a large Stone directly in Form and Manner like the *Tripos's* which in those Days of Ignorance, the Priests stood upon, to deliver their fabulous Oracles

Thro' one of these old Churches, there was formerly a Passage to the Apartment belonging to the Captain of the Guard, but is now closed up. The Reason they give you for it, is a pretty odd one; but as I think it not sufficient Satisfaction to my curious Reader, to acquaint him with what sort of Buildings this Island affords, without letting him know also what Traditions are concerning them, I shall have little Regard to the Censure of those Criticks, who find fault with every thing out of the common Road; and in this, as well as in all other Places, where it falls in my Way, shall make it my Endeavour to lead him into the Humours and very Souls of the *Manks* People.

They

They fay, that an Apparition called, in their Language, the *Mauthe Doog*, in the fhape of a laige black Spaniel with curled fhaggy Hair, was ufed to haunt *Peel* Caftle, and has been frequently feen in every Room, but particularly in the Guard-Chamber, where, as foon as Candles were lighted, it came and lay down before the Fire in prefence of all the Soldiers, who at length, by being fo much accuftomed to the Sight of it, loft great Part of the Terror they were feized with at its firft Appearance. They ftill however, retain'd a certain Awe, as believing it was an Evil Spirit which only waited Permiffion to do them Hurt, and for that Reafon, forbore Swearing and all prophane Difcourfe while in its Company. But tho' they indured the Shock of fuch a Gueft when all together in a Body, none cared to be left alone with it: it being the Cuftom, therefore, for one of the Soldiers to lock the Gates of the Caftle at a certain Hour, and carry them to the Captain, to whofe Apartment, as I faid before, the Way led thro' a Church; they agreed among themfelves, that whoever was to fucceed the enfuing Night, his fellow in this Errand fhould accompany him that went firft, and by this means, no Man would be expos'd fingly to the Danger: for I forgot to mention that the *Mauthe Doog* was always feen to come from that Paffage at the Clofe of Day, and return to it again as foon as the Morning dawned; which made them look on this Place as its peculiar Refidence.

One Night a Fellow being drunk, and by the ftength of his Liquor rendered more daring than ordinary, laugh'd at the Simplicity of his Companions, and tho' it was not his Turn to go with

B 3   the

the Keys, would needs take that Office upon him, to teftify his Courage. All the Soldiers endeavoured to diffuade him, but the more they faid, the more refolute he feem'd, and fwore that he defired nothing more than that *Mauthe Doog* would follow him, as it had done the others, for he would try if it were Dog or Devil. After having talked in a very reprobate Manner for fome Time, he fnatched up the Keys and went out of the Guard-Room : in fome Time after his Departure a great Noife was heard, but no body had the Boldnefs to fee what occafioned it, till the Adventurer returning, they demanded the Knowledge of him; but as loud and noify as he had been at leaving them, he was now become fober and filent enough, for he was never heard to fpeak more · and tho' all the Time he lived, which was three Days, he w. entreated by all who came near him, either to fpeak or if he could not do that, to make fome Signs, by which they might underftand what had happened to him, yet nothing intelligible could be got from him, only, that by the Diftortion of his Limbs and Features, it might be guefs'd that he died in Agonies more than is common in a natural Death.

The *Mauthe Doog* was, however, never feen after in the Caftle, nor would any one attempt to go thro' that Paffage, for which Reafon it was clofed up and another Way made. This Accident happened about 60 Years fince, and I heard it attefted by feveral, but efpecially by an old Soldier, who affured me he had feen it oftner than he had the Hairs on his Head.

Having taken Notice of every thing remarkable in the Churches, I believe my Reader will be impatient to come to the Caftle itfelf, which, in fp of the Magnificence the Pride of modern Ages has adorned the Palaces of Princes with, exceeds not only every thing I have seen, but also read of, in Nobleness of Structure. Tho' now no more than a Garrison for Soldiers, you cannot enter into it without being struck with a Veneration, which the most beautiful Buildings of latter Years cannot inspire you with; the Largeness and Loftiness of the Rooms, the vast Eccho resounding thro' them, the many winding Galleries, the Prospect of the Sea, and the Ships, which by reason of the Height of the Place, seem but like Buoys floating on the Waves, makes you fancy yourself in a superior Orb to what the rest of Mankind inhabit, and fills you with Contemplations the most refined and pure that the Soul is capable of conceiving.

The Situation, Strength, and Magnificence of this Edifice, inclines me very much to believe what the Natives say it was built for, the Education of young Princes, for certainly Study and Meditation can no where be more indulged. Happy were it for the Youth of *England*, if our Universities had the same Advantage, so many of our Nobility and Gentry would not then imbibe a Corruption of Morals with an Improvement of Learning.

It was in this Castle that *Eleanor*, Wife to *Humphrey* Duke of *Gloucester*, Uncle to King *Henry* VI. and Lord Protector of *England*, was confined, after being banished thro' the Malice of the Duke of *Suffolk*, and Cardinal of *Winchester*, who accused her of having been guilty of associating herself with Wizards and Witches, to know if her Husband would ever attain the Crown, and other treasonable Practices. Sir *John Stanley* then Lord of *Man*, had the Charge of her, and having conduct-

ed

ed her to the Island, placed her in this Castle ; where she lived in a Manner befitting her Dignity, nothing but Liberty being refused : she appeared however so turbulent and impatient under this Confinement, that he was obliged to keep a Guard over her, not only because there were daily Attempts made to get her away, but also to prevent her from laying violent Hands on her own Life. They tell you, that ever since her Death, to this Hour, a Person is heard to go up the stone Stairs of one of these little Houses on the Walls, constantly every Night as soon as the Clock has struck Twelve ; but I never heard any one say they had seen what it was, tho' the general Conjecture is, that it is no other than the troubled Spirit of this Lady, who died, as she had lived, dissatisfied, and murmuring at her Fate.

I could dwell much longer on the Description of a Place which I so much admire , but I fear being tedious, and shall therefore conduct my Reader from the Castle to the Town, which is long, but narrow, few People of any Distinction dwelling here most of the Houses are but a better sort of Cabins. Here is a very good Harbour, and much resorted by the *Scotch* and *Irish* Vessels, being the nearest to them.

Ramsay is the next Town of Note, and the Inhabitants, as the Buildings, are a degree genteeler than those of *Peel* ; but has no great matter in it, worthy the Observation of a Traveller, except an excellent Harbour and good Fort.

Nor has *Ballasalhe* any thing to boast of, beside a fine River running thro' it, a good Air to whiten Cloth, and a Market for Fowls, where you may have the greatest Choice of any Place in the Island.

Macguires,

Macguires, or *New-Town*, was a waſte Piece of
Ground, till after his late Majeſty's Acceſſion to
the Crown ; when one *Macguire*, a Native of *Ireland*, and Tenant to Lord *Darby*, built a large
Houſe on it for himſelf, and ſeveral little ones to
let out at yearly Rent. 'Tis yet, however, no
more than a Village, but in Compliment to him
is called a Town, and after his Name : it is in a
pleaſant and convenient Part of the Iſland, for
which reaſon, 'tis believed, 'twill hereafter be
enlarged.

These Towns are divided into Seventeen Pariſhes, which I ſhall give you the Names of in the
Order they ſtand in the Regiſter.

Kirk Jarmyn.

Kirk Patrick.	*Kirk Lennon.*
Kirk Michaell.	*Kirk Canton*
Kirk Ballaugh.	*Kirk Braddon.*
Kirk Jurby.	*Kirk Maroan.*
Kirk Bride.	*Kirk Santon.*
Kirk Candras.	*Kirk Merlugh.*
Kirk Chriſtleſare.	*Kirk Caſtra.*
Kirk Mahal	*Kirk Chriſt-Ruſſin,*

When Dr *Wilſon*, Biſhop of *Man*, was about
publiſhing his ſhort, but exact Account of the Iſl-
nd, he ordered all his Parochial Clergy to ſend
im a Liſt of the Number of Souls, including
ſtrangers, in their reſpective Pariſhes, which at
that Time amounted to no more than 14,500 tho'
through a Miſtake of the Printer the Number
publiſhed, was 15,000 ; but ſince that, ſo many
uſh Families have come over and ſettled there,
that the Account is greatly encreaſed.

As

As to their Laws, they are but few, but severely executed, especially, as I before observed, those of the Ecclesiastick Court, the Clergy holding a kind of tyrannical Jurisdiction over the *Manks* People, in spite of the temporal Power, which is continually endeavouring to abate the Rigor of it, but in vain: for these spiritual Masters are, in a manner, idolized by the Natives, and they take care to maintain their Authority by keeping the Laity in the most miserable Ignorance: not that this is altogether Policy, for he cannot well instruct, who wants to be taught himself. What eminent Men this Island has formerly bred, I know not, but at present I hear of none famous abroad; nor can it boast of any more at home than one Clergyman, who is indeed a Man of Letters, and who, I hope, will oblige the publick with his instructive and polite Writings. He, considering the profound Ignorance of his Countrymen, for their sakes undertook a Translation of the New Testament into the *Manks* Tongue, of which Work he had (as I have been credibly informed) finished the four Gospels, and had proceeded in it, if the Publication thereof had not been prohibited by a superior Power. Books written in the *Manks* Tongue, they have none, except a Catechism, and Instructions for Youth, with some Prayers not many Years since compiled.

Some who are willing to entertain the most favourable Opinion of this People, impute their general Ignorance to their Want of Books: but I, who have lived and conversed some Time among them, attribute their Want of Books to their innate Ignorance. That this Suggestion is not without Grounds, appears from the little Progress

made

made in Learning by thofe who have had the happy Advantage of finifhing their Education in an
Irifh or *Scotch* College, which is commonly the
Cafe of fuch as are defigned for Holy Orders;
notwithftanding which, we find none of their Writings made publick, nor would moft of their Sermons pafs on any but a *Manks* Congregation. If
to this they object that their Language is obfcure,
and not well known in the World, let them write
(as they frequently preach) in *Englifh*, or in *Latin*,
a Language univerfally known to the learned World.
To prevent Controverfies and fupport their impe-
rious Sway, the Clergy (like thofe of the Church
of *Rome*) hold the Laity under blind abject Obedience; of which take this Inftance: When I
once, in Converfation with two young Clergymen,
lamented the abovementioned Prohibition, which
debar'd the common People (who fpeak only their
own Language) from the delightful Benefit, and
neceffary Duty of fearching the Scriptures, they
agreed in this Anfwer, That it was happy for the
People that the Scriptures were lock'd up from
them, for it prevented Divifions in the Interpreta-
tion of them, which was given to themfelves, and
to themfelves only, by their Great Dictator, who
had fubftituted them as Vicars and the Interpre-
ters of his Law. It may, perhaps, not be unworthy the Confideration of that Power which prefides
over the Diocefs of *Man*, whether the greater Inconvenience accrues from a Publication, or a Suppreffion of the Tranflation I fpeak of? In the firft
Cafe, what is objected by the Clergymen is not
without fome Grounds, *viz.* that fuch a Tranflation would lay the Scriptures open to the different
Interpretations of ignorant, prejudiced, or evil-
defigning

defigning Men, and raife Difputes even in Matters
of Faith, carried on in a Language ftrange to their
Metropolitan, nay even to their Diocefan , by
which means the unfpotted Difcipline of the Church
might be polluted, her pure Doctrine corrupted,
the Laws of God perverted or broken, his Holy
Name blafphemed, and yet the great Offender ef-
cape unpunifhed, nay, untry'd. Yet for all this,
fuch a Tranflation is earneftly to be defired, when
we confider the miferable Condition of that unhappy People, who, furrounded by the moft learned Nations of *Europe*, remain in a State of utter
Ignorance, and rather imitate than conform to'the
pureft Church of God upon Earth. They hear the
Scriptures read, but not expounded, every Sab-
bath. Their Prayer-Books and Bibles are printed
in *Englifh*, and the Minifter mentally tranflates
the Service into the *Manks* Tongue, as he delivers
it to the People. From thefe two Confiderations
I draw this Queftion, as before mentioned, Whether the greater Inconvenience or Evil accrues from
a Publication or Suppreffion of a Tranflation ? On
the one hand there would be a fix'd, certain, known
Rule of Faith of which the People might in another Generaton be brought to comprehend, that
is, if thofe who ought to inftruct them would do
it) and by which they would be govern'd. As the
Cafe now ftands, they are directed by the various
Interpretations of various Preachers , nay, by the
various Interpretations of one Preacher ; for who
can fuppofe that any Man fhall at all Times (tho'
on the fame Subject) ufe the fame Expreffions,
Words, or Terms. Does not this Method open a
Door to that endlefs Confufion, which fome think
they prudently exclude by prohibiting the Publication.

tion. Besides, without being accounted malicious, would not any difinterefted Perfon ask the Quefti-on, why thefe People are fo ignorant, why there is not better Care taken in forming their Youth? But I fhall add no more on this Head, left I be thought by fome (whofe earthly and fpiritual Wel-fare I heartily wifh) too bufily concerned in an Af-fair which they may think foreign to me, but let them confider, *Chriftianus fum, Chriftiani nihil a me alienum puto.* Leaving then this Queftion, I fhall fay fomething of their Method of inftructing the People, young and old.

Firft, of their Schools: The Mafters of them are generally chofen out of the Clergy: how im-properly the Motto over St. *Paul*'s School, *Ingre-dere ut Proficies*, would fuit one of thefe, may be eafily concluded from the Character of the Learn-ing of thefe temporal Mafters, but as no more is reafonably to be expected from any Man than he is capable of performing, the great Deficiency in the Scholaftick Part of the Education of Youth here, we will, in Charity, rather reckon a Mif-fortune than a Fault or Neglect in the Teachers. Yet one Error, and that an enormous one, I can-not omit mentioning, that they admit into their fchools the Children of Papifts, as it were, for no other purpofe than to keep them in Ignorance, taking fo little regard of them, that like Betrayers of their Profeffion in every Capacity, they fuffer them to go on in Blindnefs, and divert themfelves with Fables or Legends, while other Boys of the fame Age, are inftructed in an Explanation of the Church Catechifm, publifh'd in *Englifh* and *Manks* for that purpofe, and are every Sunday publickly examined therein in their refpective Churches or

Chapels;

Chapels; in which Places, the former are wholly
exempted from ever appearing. The Methods
made use of by the Popish Priests, to continue under their heavy and intolerable Yoke, the ignorant Vulgar, are called *Pious Frauds*; their Labours in converting Men of different Communions,
a *Pious Zeal*. This Clergy have also their *Frauds*,
but want the *Zeal*. They neither plant, nor water, nor pray to God for Increase of the true Faith.
They are so far from suppressing Popery in its In-
fancy, that they even educate Youth under those
mistaken Principles, by which Means it takes such
deep Root in the Adult, and is so cultivated and
corroborated by the Neglect of the sleepy Servant,
and the Diligence of the Enemy, that it becomes
irradicable in unbending old Age. Another dangerous Inconvenience arising from hence, is, the
frequent Opportunities which the Popish Children
have of corrupting, irretrievably corrupting, the
tender Principles of their Protestant School-Fel-
lows. Let no Man censure me, that I have used
Words so harsh as *irretrievably corrupting*; which
Expression may easily be allowed me, when the
Indolence and Inabilities of these School-Masters
are considered. Are not these Men then those
wicked ones, who, in effect, sow the Tares among
the Wheat?

After what I have said of the temporal Masters, let
me add to them the spiritual Pastors, equally negli-
gent and equally guilty It is most notorious that some
Popish Priest or other, is sent over thither once, twice,
or oftner in a Year, and there exercise their Function,
in private Houses, in all its Branches. They do
not indeed expose themselves to the Penalties of
the Laws (if yet there be any penal Law against
them

them in that Island) by going about to make Con-
verts; their Conversation when amongst Protes-
tants, is free and open on general Subjects. They
confine themselves much among their own People,
and leave this dirty dangerous Work to their
Slaves, the bigotted Laity, by frequently inculca-
ting into them the necessary Duty imply'd in their
perverted Explanation of the two last Verses of
the general Epistle of St. *James, viz. Brethren, if
any of you do err from the Truth, and one convert
him, let him know that he which converteth the
Sinner from the Error of his Way, shall save a Soul
from Death, and shall hide a Multitude of Sins.*
Hence arise those Bickerings, those Railings, those
Backbitings, and Animosities, which infest this
Isle, and disturb the Tranquillity of it. This great
Evil, and its Cause and Original, was lately com-
plained of (the Bishop being then in *England*) to
the Vicar-General, by some Protestant *English*
Gentlemen, who offered to prove that a Popish
Priest then resided and officiated at *Duglas*; desi-
ring, that if Confinement, and a legal Trial were
deemed too severe, he might at least be dismiss'd,
before the Contagion of his Doctrine should spread
too far. This Complaint, and Petition, tho' often repeated, were absolutely rejected by the Vicar-General: and the Priest went on (so long as
he thought fit) without fear or Molestation. Are
these Men the true Pastors? Are not these the
Hirelings who flee through Fear, and leave the
sheep committed to their Care a Prey to the ra-
vening Wolf?

Over the elder People of the Island, these Men
reign with the joined Power of spiritual Pastors and
Masters. their Injunctions, for they cannot pro-

properly

perly be called Inftructions, are delivered from the Pulpit in Harangues, which go by the Denomination of Sermons, in which are never heard the divine Attributes afterted, or any Article of Faith proved from Scripture, fometimes, indeed, they preach up a Moral Duty, but the chief and moft frequent Subject of their Difcourfes, is the Power of the Priefthood, and the Difcipline of the Church. Thefe Doctrines they thunder out, as the Pope does his Bulls, with an Anathema tacked to them, and enforce them by a ftrong Argument called *Kirk Jarmyns*, on all who are difobedient or unbelieving: for proof of which, I appeal to an *Englifh* Gentleman, who not long fince was fentenced to that horrid Prifon, I before defcribed (under the *Bifhop*'s Chapel in *Peel* Caftle) by a fpiritual Court for barely feeming to fuppofe that one of the Brotherhood was not overftocked with Learning. A Summons was ferved upon the Gentleman before the Sentence *was* regiftred, (nor indeed *is it yet*) and he had certainly been fent to Prifon, and ordered to do Penance, but that he declared he appeal'd to the Metropolitan, or challeng'd his Antagonift to difprove his Affertion before the beft Judges of Learning his Country could produce Upon this, the Minifter, by the Advice of his Brethren, confcious of the Weaknefs of his Caufe, dropt the Profecution, and has ever fince fat down as contentedly under the Character of an Illiterate, as a Bully does under a Beating.

The Difcipline of the Church being perpetually dinn'd into the Ears of the Laity, and the indifpenfable Obligation of fubmitting to it, the abject Creatures are drove to Prifon like Sheep to Fold, and from thence to publick Penance, as quickly quietly as thofe Beafts are to the Slaughter: deterred, on the one Hand, from Murmuring, by the Threatnings of feverer Punifhments; and perfuaded on the other, that patient Submiffion to the Inflictors is the fupremeft Merit in the Eyes of Heaven

How little the Methods taken by this Court to prevent Fornication have fucceeded, may be known by the great Number of Offenders, which are every *Sunday* doing Penance for it in theirChurches; and in my Opinion, draw on a more pernicious Evil than that which they defign to avoid. If the leaft Famiharity is obferved between Perfons of a different Sex, they are immediately fummon'd to the Communion-Table, and there obliged to fwear themfelves innocent, or endure the Shame and Punithment ordained for the Crime of Fornication. This they call *Purging*, but it is fo far from being worthy of that Name, that many to avoid public Difgrace, add the Sin of Perjury to the other, and take the moft folemn Oath that can be invented to a Falfhood. Innumerable are the Inftances I could give of this Truth, but to avoid being tedious, I fhall repeat but one, that being of fo dreadful a Nature, as may very well ferve to convince my Reader, that too much Severity, as well as too much Lenity, is of dangerous Confequence. A Widow at *Duglas*, being of a light Behaviour, was frequently fufpected to be guilty of Fornication, and accordingly was fummon'd, and took the Oath of Purgation, (how truly, the Sequel will prove) As fhe was one Evening going home, fhe was accofted by a Stranger, I think he was of *Wales*, and Mafter of a Veffel; what Difcourfe paffed between them is unknown, nor is it of

much

much Confequence, any farther than that they a-
greed to go together to her Lodging, where, having made him very drunk, fhe rifled his Pocket
of Ten Guineas, then made a Pretence to get him
down Stairs. but he no fooner came into the Air,
then it deprived him of all the little Senfe the Liquor had left him ; and being unable to reel any
farther, he lay down at the Door, and fell into a
found Sleep When waked, he miffed his Money,
he remember'd the Encounter he had had with
the Woman, but could not be certain if fhe had
taken it from him, or whether he might not have
been robbed as he was afleep On relating the
Story however, to his Landlady, fhe perfuaded
him to make his Complaint, and procure Leave
to fearch the Lodgings of this Woman. The Ad
vice was followed, and the Officers, being very
diligent in their Scrutiny, found in her Bofom one
Guinea, under a heap of Afhes a fecond, and good
Part of the Change of another. As fhe was ex
tremely poor, and had nothing to fubfift on, but what
fhe got by daily Labour from Houfe to Houfe,
'twas eafy to believe this was none of her own Mo
ney ; they therefore doubted not but they fhould
find the Remainder of what the Captain had loft
which indeed they did, and with it a much more
fhocking Difcovery, in turning up the Bed : there
lay under it a Parcel of fmall Bones, which feem
ing to be human, they fent immediately for two
Doctors, the one named *Jenkenfon*, the other *Bull*
who, on joining them together, made the perfect
Anatomies of three Children , the Back-Bone of
one of them, had been cleft through, as it feemed
with a Hatchet. Every one was ftruck with the
utmoft Horrour at this Sight, except the inhuman

Mothe

Mother and Murdrefs, who impudently owned they were all her own Children, which she had been delivered of in private, to avoid Punishment, but pretended in her Defence that they were still-born. She was then asked, why she did not bury them? To which she answered, that was not the Business of any body, they were her own; and being dead, she might difpofe of them as she pleas'd. Perhaps, added she, I had a mind to keep them by me for the Sake of those who begot them.

She was, however, carried to Prifon, under the double Indictment of Theft and Murder; and being unable to alledge any thing in her Juftifica-tion, was condemned to Death, and accordingly executed 'Twas remarkable that this Wretch, when under Sentence, being asked why she had not buried the Children, fince she might have eafily had an Opportunity? told the Perfon who made his Demand, that defigning to throw them into the River, she took up the Bones in her A- on one Night, but as she was going, was met by a tall black Gentleman, who bid her go back; adding, she was fafe while she kept them at home, but if she attempted to conceal them either in Earth or Water, she would certainly be difcovered.

Whether this miferable Creature faw any fuch Apparition or not, or whether it was the Will of God that she should imagine she faw and heard that in effect was nothing, I will not pretend to determine; but it is plain that Divine Juftice,who feldom fuffers Murder to go unpunifhed, even on earth, was very vifible in compelling her to take the only Means which could detect her.

But to return, tho' the Defign in the firft Infti-tion of *Purging* was certainly good, and may de-

ter

ter thofe who confider the Danger of taking a falfe Oath, and calling the fupreme Name of God to witnefs an Untruth, from entering into any unwarrantable Engagement; yet when there is fo little Care taken by the Priefthood, to infpire a juft Notion of Things, as I before faid, it ferves rather to add Sin to Sin, by fuffering thefe poor Ignorants to enhance their future Punifhment, in avoiding the prefent one

Here I think it may be convenient to clear my felf from any Reflections which may be caft on me as a Cenfurer of Church Difcipline, I acknowledge (as every Member of the Church of *England* ought) that in the Primitive Church there was a godly Difcipline, that at the Beginning of *Lent*, fuch Perfons as ftood convicted of notorious Sins were put to open Penance: and farther, I join with the Church, in wifhing that the faid Difcipline may be reftored again: nay, I would not be thought to confine fuch Penance to any particular Seafon of the Year, but think the Punifhment fhou'd be inflicted at a convenient Diftance of Time after the Conviction of the Offender. To the Doctrines of our Holy Church, the exprefs Law of God, I pay entire Obedience: to her Difcipline, the Inftitution of Men, not repugnant to the former, nor corrupted by Innovations, I fubmit. fo, on the other hand, all illegally affumed Power, all tyrannical and unjuft Cenfures, and Sentences ecclefiaftical, I fhall with my utmoft Endeavours oppofe, not doubting but fuch arbitrary Judicature will in Time prove as fatal to the Church, as in the laft Age a pretended High Court of Juftice was to the *Monarchy*. But as I poffibly may have occafion to fpeak more of this Head elfewhere, I fhall leave it it here for the present, and obferve what Advances they make toward eftablifhing their Hierarchy from their other Doctrine, *viz.* the Power of the Priefthood. And this is, indeed, their Corner-ftone, the Foundation on which the ftupendous ftructure is erected to fuch a gigantic and formidable Heighth, moft exactly framed after the Model fet before them their Grand Mafters, the *Romifh* Clergy. How eafy is it to mifguide the Stranger, or delude the Ignorant? Would the *Moors* fear their Emperors, or the *Egyptians* pay fuch Adoration to their *Sultans*, as at this Day we fee they do, were they not made to believe implicitely that there is a Divinity in the Perfons of thofe abfolute Tyrants? Nor do the Men I fpeak of, exercife lefs Domination over their People, forgetting the Words of our Saviour, that, *Bleffed are the meek in Spirit*, they look, and move, and fpeak, as if they knew themfelves to be of a different Spece from their Hearers, and frown them into that Awe, and Reverence, which they ought to acquire only by a Superiority of Goodnefs. I heard an old Man fay, that a certain Chaplain, (who fhall be namelefs, left any one fhould think I mingle Prejudice with Truth) ought to be honoured as God upon Earth, and that as fuch he would always honour him. But this poor Man has lived to fee his Error, for this God whom he would have worfhipped, was foon after detected of a Crime for which he was obliged to quit the Ifland, to avoid the Punifhment the Law ordains for it. If any Man think me to blame, or that I pay not due Deference to the facerdotal Function, I anfwer, that the Church of *England* commands me fo proceed, fee Article of Religion 26.----*It appertaineth*

perta neth to the *Discipline of the Church, that* E...
quiry be made of evil Ministers, and that they be a...
cused by those who have Knowledge of their Offences
and finally, being found guilty, by just Judgment h...
deposed. The Church enjoins all those, withou...
Limitation, who have Knowledge of Offences, t...
accuse the Offenders, but since this brow-beate...
Laity rather conceal than disclose the Enormiti...
of their Ministry, evil Ministers I might well c...
them, since, as 'tis proved, they admit the Wo...
among the Sheep, I think it more particularly...
Duty incumbent on me, (who am not only a Sub...
ject, but a Servant also in this Place, to his pre...
sent, as I was to his late sac ed Majesty) to brin...
these Things to the Knowledge of those, who...
Intent and Inclination, I doubt not, is, to ou...
just Judgment. And since all private Accusation...
tending to obtain this Justice, have been (as is be...
fore related) rejected or suppress'd, it is now hig...
Time to exhibit this publick one. Thus, n...
many Years since, when the arbitrary Proceeding...
of a powerful Man, and the Oppressions whic...
one of our Universities groan'd under, were be...
come insupportable; Redress was loudly, th...
humbly, sued for, in a Representation of the Sta...
of that University made publick by a late emine...
Lawyer, and in a most pathetic Letter from...
learned and a truly reverend Divine, to his Patro...
possess'd of a high Station in the Administration...
Justice. And tho' they did not succeed in the...
intended Reformation, by bringing a Royal Vi...
tation on that University, (the Distraction of tho...
Times then probably preventing, and the a...
Behaviour of that Body perhaps averting it)...
were the commendable Labours of those Gent...

...n amply rewarded, by the fignal Honours
...ich each in his refpective Profeffion received;
...fide that innate Happinefs, which diffufes itfelf
...o' the Soul when confcious of having done, or
...empted to do a good Action. This laft, what-
...r may be my Expectations of the former, will
...ainly be my Portion, and abundantly make up
...whatever Malice may be conceived againft me
...thofe whofe Deeds being evil, fhun the Light.
...But as it is no lefs, if not a greater Error, to
...it the Praifes of the good, than to lay open,
...warn Men of unworthy Paftors, I muft not
...t this Subject without mentioning fome of thofe
...ny amiable Qualities, which adorn the Charac-
...of the prefent *Bifhop*. Long, and uninterrup-
...Cuftom has made the Spiritual Court of fuch
...arbitrary Authority, that fhould he derogate
...m it, he would be in great Danger of publick
...pofition, as well as private Hatred, from the
...ole Body of inferior Clergy : he therefore may
...faid rather to comply with, than approve of it,
...ng in his own Nature, what our bleffed Saviour
...mmends, mild, humble, tender, compaffionate,
...forgiving. But the abundant Charities he be-
...vs, and which we too well know, not to have
...hed whereever this Treatife will arrive, are bet-
...Teftimonials of him than the Words of any
...thor. Some few, but alas ! they are but few,
...he Vicars and Chaplains, may alfo be exempt-
...rom the general Character above given.
...s the Earl of *Derby*, tho' ftiled *Lord of Man*,
...ht juftly enough be called *King*, all Caufes, ex-
...in the Spiritual Court, being tryed in his
...me, and all Warrants for Life and Death figned
...is Hand; his utmoft Endeavours have not

been

been wanting to curb the assuming Power of the Ecclesiasticks. As for Example, when the Summner comes to apprehend any Person for an Offence committed, or said to be committed in that Court, had the Person so seized, Courage enough to refuse going to Prison under his Conduct, he cannot be compelled, because the Soldiers of the Garrison have Orders from their Commanders never to be aiding nor assisting to any such Commitments. Hence it follows, that the spiritual and temporal Powers are at the extremest Odds with each other; and were it not for the blind Obedience the Laity pay to their Ghostly Fathers, the former would soon be subjected.

'Tis this Ignorance which is the Occasion of the excessive Superstition which reigns among them. I have already given some Hints of it, but not enough to show the World what a *Monks* Man truly is, and what Power the Prejudice of Education has over weak Minds. If Books were of any Use among them, one would swear the Count of *Gabalis* had been not only translated into the *Monk* Tongue, but that it was a sort of Rule of Faith to them, since there is no fictious Being mentioned by him, in his Book of Absurdities, which they would not readily give credit to. I know not, Idolize as they are of the Clergy, whether they would not be even refractory to them, were they to preach against the Existence of *Fairies*, or even against their being commonly seen; for tho' the Priesthood are a kind of Gods among them, yet still Tradition is a greater God than they, and as they confidently assert that the first Inhabitants of their Island were *Fairies*, so do they maintain that these little People have still their Residence among them: Ji

call them *the good People*, and say they live in
Wilds and Forests, and on Mountains, and shun
great Cities because of the Wickedness acted therein, all the Houses are blessed where they visit, for
they fly Vice. A Person would be thought impudently prophane, who should suffer his Family to
go to Bed without having first set a Tub, or Pail
full of clean Water, for these Guests to bathe themselves in, which the Natives aver they constantly
do, as soon as ever the Eyes of the Family are
closed, whenever they vouchsafe to come. If any
thing happen to be mislaid, and found again, in
some Place where it was not expected, they pre-
sently tell you a *Fairy* took it and return'd it : if
you chance to get a Fall, and hurt yourself, a *Fairy*
laid something in your Way to throw you down,
a Punishment for some Sin you have committed.
I have heard many of them protest they have
been carried insensibly great Distances from home,
and, without knowing how they came there, found
themselves on the Top of a Mountain. One Story
in particular, was told me of a Man who had been
led by invisible Musicians for several Miles together, and not being able to resist the Harmony,
followed till it conducted him to a large Common,
where were a great Number of little People sitting
round a Table, and eating and drinking in a very
jovial manner· Among them were some Faces whom
he thought he had formerly seen, but forbore taking any notice, or they of him, till the little People offering him Drink, one of them, whose
features seemed not unknown to him, plucked
him by the Coat, and forbad him, whatever
he did, to taste any thing he saw before him ;
for if you do, added he, you will be as I am, and

D   *return*

return no more to your Family. The poor Man was much affrighted, but refolved to obey the Injunction : accordingly a large filver Cup filled with fome fort of Liquor, being put into his Hand, he found an Opportunity to throw what it contained on the Ground. Soon after the Mufick ceafing, all the Company difappeared, leaving the Cup in his Hand , and he returned home, tho' much wearied and fatigued. He went the next Day, and communicated to the Minifter of the Parifh all that had happened, and asked his Advice how he fhould difpofe of the Cup : to which the Parfon reply'd, he could not do better than to devote it to the Service of the Church ; and this very Cup, they tell me, is that which is now ufed for the confecrated Wine in *Kirk-Merlugh.*

Another Inftance they gave me to prove the Reality of *Fairies,* was of a Fidler, who having agreed with a Perfon, who was a Stranger, for fo much Money, to play to fome Company he fhould bring him to, all the twelve Days of *Chriftmafs,* and received Earneft for it, faw his new Mafter vanifh into the Earth the Moment he had made the Bargain. Nothing could be more terrified than was the poor Fidler ; he found he had entered himfelf into the Devil's Service, and looked on himfelf as already damned ; but having recourfe alfo to a Clergyman, he received fome Hope : he ordered him however, as he had taken Earneft, to go when he fhould be called ; but that whatever Tunes fhould be called for, to play none but Pfalms. On the Day appointed, the fame Perfon appeared, with whom he went, tho' with what inward Reluctance 'tis eafy to guefs ; but punctually obeying the Minifter's Directions, the Company to whom he

play'd

play'd were fo angry, that they all vaniſhed at once, leaving him at the Top of a high Hill, and ſo bruiſed and hurt, tho' he was not ſenſible when, or from what Hand he received the Blows, that he got not home without the utmoſt Difficulty.

The old Story of Infants being changed in their Cradles, is here in ſuch Credit, that Mothers are in continual Terror at the Thoughts of it. I was prevailed upon myſelf, to go and ſee a Child, who, they told me was one of theſe Changelings, and indeed muſt own was not a little ſurprized, as well as ſhocked at the Sight: nothing under Heaven could have a more beautiful Face: but tho' between Five and Six Years old, and ſeemingly healthy, he was ſo far from being able to walk, or ſtand, that he could not ſo much as move any one Joint: his Limbs were vaſtly long for his Age, but ſmaller than an Infant's of ſix Months; his Complexion was perfectly delicate, and he had the fineſt Hair in the World; he never ſpoke nor cryed, eat ſcarce any thing, and was very ſeldom ſeen to ſmile, but if any one called him a *Fairy Elf*, he would frown, and ſet his Eyes ſo earneſtly on thoſe who ſaid it, as if he would look them through. His Mother, or at leaſt his ſuppoſed Mother, being very poor, frequently went out a Chairing, and left him a whole Day together: The Neighbours, out of Curioſity, have often looked in at the Window to ſee how he behaved when alone, which whenever they did, they were ſure to find him laughing, and in the moſt Delight. This made them judge that he was without Company more pleaſing to him than any Mortal's could be; and what made this Conjecture ſeem the more reaſonable, was, that if he were left ever ſo dirty, the Woman, at her Re-

turn

turn, faw him with a clean Face, and his Hair combed with the utmoſt Exactneſs and Nicety.

A ſecond Account of this Nature, I had from a Woman to whoſe Offspring the *Fairies* ſeemed to have taken a particularFancy. The 4th or 5thNight after ſhe was delivered of her firſt Child, the Family were alarm'd with a moſt terrible Cry of Fire; on which, every body run out of the Houſe to ſee whence it proceeded, not excepting the Nurſe, who being much frighted as the others, made one of the Number. The poor Woman lay trembling in her Bed, alone, unable to help herſelf, and her Back being turned to the Infant, ſaw not that it was taken away by an inviſible Hand. Thoſe who had left her, having enquired about the Neighbourhood, and finding there was no Cauſe for the Out-cry they had heard, laugh'd at each other for the Miſtake, but as they were going to re-enter the Houſe, the poor Babe lay on the Threſhold and by its Cries preſerv'd itſelf from being trod upon. This exceedingly amazed all that ſaw it, and the Mother being ſtill in Bed, they could aſſign no Reaſon for finding it there, but having been removd by *Fairies*, who, by their ſudden Return had been prevented from carrying it any farther.

About a Year after, the ſame Woman was brought to Bed of a Second Child, which had not been born many Nights before a great Noiſe was heard in the Houſe where they kept their Cattle (for in this Iſland, where there is no Shelter in the Fields from the exceſſive Cold and Damps, they put all their Milch Kine into a Barn, which they call a Cattle-Houſe.) Every body that was ſtirring, ran to ſee what was the matter, believing that the Cows had got looſe. the Nurſe was as re

dy as the reſt, but finding all ſafe, and the Barn-
Door cloſe, immediately returned, but not ſo ſuddenly but that the new-born Babe was taken out
of the Bed, as the former had been, and dropt on
their Coming, in the Middle of the Entry. This
was enough to prove the *Fairies* had made a ſecond
attempt, and the Parents ſending for a Miniſter,
join'd with him in Thankſgiving to God, who had
twice delivered their Children from being taken
from them.

But in the Time of her Third Lying-in, every
body ſeem'd to have forgot what had happened in
the Firſt and Second, and on a Noiſe in the Cattle-Houſe ran out to know what had occaſioned it.
The Nurſe was the only Perſon, excepting the
Woman in the Straw, who ſtayed in the Houſe,
nor was ſhe detained thro' Care, or Want of Curioſity, but by the Bonds of Sleep, having drank a
little too plentifully the preceding Day. The
Mother, who was broad awake, ſaw her Child
lifted out of the Bed, and carried out of the Chamber, tho' ſhe could not ſee any Perſon touch it, on
which, ſhe cryed out as loud as ſhe could, Nurſe,
Nurſe! my Child, my Child is taken away; but
the old Woman was too faſt, to be awaken'd by
the Noiſe ſhe made, and the Infant was irretriev-
bly gone. When her Husband, and thoſe who
had accompany'd him, return'd, they found her
wringing her Hands and uttering the moſt piteous
Lamentations for the Loſs of her Child: on which
ſaid the Husband, looking into the Bed, the Woman is mad, do not you ſee the Child lies by you?
on which ſhe turned, and ſaw ſomething indeed like
a Child, but far different from her own, who was a
very beautiful, fat, well-featured Babe; whereas what

was

was now in the room of it, was a poor, lean, withered, deformed Creature. It lay quite naked, but the Cloaths belonging to the Child that was exchanged for it, lay wrapt up altogether on the Bed.

This Creature lived with them near the Space of nine Years, in all which Time it eat nothing except a few Herbs, nor was ever seen to void any other Excrement than Water: it neither spoke, nor could stand or go, but seemed enervate in every Joint, like the Changeling I mentioned before, and in all its Actions shewed itself to be of the same Nature.

A Woman who lived about two Miles distant from *Ballasalla*, and used to serve my Family with Butter, made me once very merry with a Story she told me of her Daughter, a Girl of about ten Years old, who being sent over the Fields to the Town for a Pennyworth of Tobacco for her Father, was on the top of a Mountain surrounded by a great Number of little Men, who would not suffer her to pass any farther. Some of them said she should go with them, and accordingly laid hold of her; but one seeming more pitiful, desired they would let her alone; which they refusing, there ensued a Quarrel, and the Person who took her Part, fought bravely in her Defence. This so incensed the others, that to be revenged on her for being the Cause, two or three of them seized her, and pulling up her Cloaths, whipped her heartily; after which, it seems, they had no farther Power over her, and she run home directly, telling what had befallen her, and shewing her Buttocks, on which were the Prints of several small Hands. Several of the Towns-People went with her to the Mountain, and she conducting them to the Spot, the little Antagonists were gone but had left behind them Proofs (as the good Woman said) that what the Girl had informed them was true; for there was a great deal of Blood to be seen on the Stones. This did she aver with all the Solemnity imaginable.

Another Woman equally superstitious and fanciful as the former, told me, that being great with Child, and expecting every Moment the good Hour, as she lay awake one Night in her Bed, she saw Seven or Eight little Women come into her Chamber, one of whom had an Infant in her Arms: they were followed by a Man of the same Size with themselves, but in the Habit of a Minister. One of them went to the Pail, and finding no Water in it, cried out to the others, What must they do to christen the Child? On which, they reply'd, it should be done in Beer. With that, the seeming Parson took the Child in his Arms, and performed the Ceremony of Baptism, dipping his Hand into a great Tub of Strong-Beer, which the Woman had brew'd the Day before to be ready for her Lying-in. She told me, that they baptized the Infant by the Name of *Joan*, which made her know she was pregnant of a Girl, as it proved a few Days after, when she was delivered. She added also, that it was common for the *Fairies* to make a Mock-Christening when any Person was near her Time, and that according to what Child, male or female, they brought, such should the Woman bring into the World.

But I cannot give over this Subject without mentioning what they say befel a young Sailor, who coming off a long Voyage, tho' it was late at Night, chose to land rather than lie another Night in the Vessel:

Veſſel : being permitted to do ſo, he was ſet on ſhore at *Duglas.* It happened to be a fine Moonlight Night, and very dry, being a ſmall Froſt, he therefore forbore going into any Houſe to refreſh himſelf, but made the beſt of his Way to the Houſe of a Siſter he had at *Kirk-Merlugh.* As he was going over a pretty high Mountain, he heard the Noiſe of Horſes, the Hollow of a Huntſman, and the fineſt Horn in the World. He was a little ſurprized that any body purſued thoſe kinds of Sports in the Night, but he had not Time for much Reflection before they all paſſed by him, ſo near that he was able to count what Number there was of them, which he ſaid, was Thirteen, and that they were all dreſt in green, and gallantly mounted. He was ſo well pleaſed with the Sight that he would gladly have follow'd, could he have kept pace with them , he croſs'd the Foot-Way, however, that he might ſee them again, which he did more than once, and loſt not the Sound of the Horn for ſome Miles. At length, being arrived at his Siſter's, he tells her the Story, who preſently clapped her Hands for Joy, that he was come home ſafe ; for, ſaid ſhe, thoſe you ſaw were *Fairies,* and 'tis well they did not take you away with them.

There is no perſuading them but that theſe Huntings are frequent in the Iſland, and that theſe little Gentry being too proud to ride on *Manks* Horſes which they might find in the Field, make uſe of the *Engliſh* and *Iriſh* ones, which are brought over and kept by Gentlemen. They ſay that nothing is more common, than to find theſe poor Beaſts in a Morning, all over in a Sweat and Foam, and tired almoſt to death, when their Owners have believed

eved they have never been out of the Stable. A
Gentleman of *Ballafletcher* affured me, he had
three or Four of his beft Horfes killed with thefe
nocturnal Journies.

At my firft coming into the Ifland, and hearing
thefe fort of Stories, I imputed the giving Credit
to them merely to the Simplicity of the poor Creatures who releated them ; but was ftrangely furprized when I heard other Narratives of this kind,
and altogether as abfurd, attefted by Men who
paffed for Perfons of found Judgment. Among
this Number, was a Gentleman my dear Neighbour, who affirmed with the moft folemn Affeve-
rations, that being of my Opinion, and entirely
averfe to the Belief that any fuch Beings were permitted to wander for the Purpofes related of them,
he had been at laft convinced by the Appearance
of feveral little Figures playing and leaping over
fome Stones in a Field, whom, a few Yards diftance he imagined were School-Boys, and intended, when he came near enough, to reprimand, for
being abfent from their Exercifes at that Time of
the Day, it being then, he faid, between Three
and Four of the Clock : but when he approached
fo near as he cou'd guefs, within Twenty Paces,
they all immediately difappeared, tho' he had never taken his Eye off them from the firft Moment
he beheld them ; nor was there any Place where
they could fo fuddenly retreat, it being an open
field without Hedge or Bufh, and, as I faid before, broad Day.

Another Inftance, which might ferve to ftrengthen the Credit of the other, was told me by a
Perfon who had the Reputation of the utmoft Integrity. This Man being defirous of difpofing of a

Horfe

Horſe he had at that Time no great Occaſion for, and riding him to Market for that Purpoſe, was accoſted, in paſſing over the Mountains, by a little Man in a plain Dreſs, who asked him if he would ſell his Horſe. 'Tis the Deſign I am going on, reply'd the Perſon who told me the Story. On which, the other deſired to know the Price. Eight Pounds, ſaid he. No, reſumed the Purchaſer, I will give no more than Seven, which, if you will take, here is your Money. The Owner thinking he had bid pretty fair, agreed with him, and the Money being told out, the one diſmounted, and the other got on the Back of the Horſe, which he had no ſooner done, than both Beaſt and Rider ſunk into the Earth immediately, leaving the Perſon who had made the Bargain in the utmoſt Terror and Conſternation. As ſoon as he had a little recovered himſelf, he went directly to the Parſon of the Pariſh, and related what had paſſed, deſiring he would give his Opinion whether he ought to make Uſe of the Money he had received, or not. To which he reply'd, that as he had made a fair Bargain, and no way circumvented, nor endeavoured to circumvent the Buyer, he ſaw no reaſon to believe, in caſe it was an evil Spirit, it could have any Power over him. On this Aſſurance, he went home well ſatisfied, and nothing afterward happened to give him any Diſquiet concerning this Affair.

A Second Account of the ſame nature I had from a Clergyman, and a Perſon of more Sanctity than the Generality of his Function in this Iſland. It was his Cuſtom to paſs ſome Hours every Evening in a Field near his Houſe, indulging Meditation, and calling himſelf to an account for the Tranſactions

ranſactions of the paſt Day. As he was in this
lace one Night more than ordinarily wrapt in
ontemplation, he wandered, without thinking
here he was, a conſiderable Way farther than it
as uſual for him to do ; and as he told me, he
new not how far the deep Muſing he was in, might
ve carried him, if it had not been ſuddenly in-
rrupted by a Noiſe, which, at firſt, he took to
the diſtant Bellowing of a Bull ; but as he liſt-
d more heedfully to it, found there was ſome-
ng more terrible in the Sound, than could pro-
d from that Creature. He confeſs'd to me, that
was no leſs affrighted than ſurprized, eſpecially
en the Noiſe coming ſtill neater, he imagined
atever it was, that it proceeded from, it muſt
s him : he had, however, Preſence enough of
nd to place himſelf with his Back to a Hedge,
re he fell on his Knees, and began to pray to
d with all the Vehemence ſo dreadful an Oc-
on required. He had not been long in that
tion, before he beheld ſomething in the Form
a Bull, but infinitely larger than ever he had
n in England, much leſs in Man, where the Cat-
are very ſmall in general. The Eyes, he ſaid
ed to ſhoot forth Flames, and the running of
as with ſuch a Force, that the Ground ſhook
er it as in an Earthquake. It made directly
ard a little Cottage, and there, after moſt hor-
roaring, diſappear'd. The Moon being then
e full, and ſhining in her utmoſt Splendor, all
e Paſſages were perfectly viſible to our amazed
ne, who having finiſhed his Ejaculations, and
Thanks to God for his Preſervation, went to
Cottage, the Owner of which, they told him,
that Moment dead. The good old Gentleman

was

was loth to pafs a Cenfure which might be judged
an uncharitable one, but the Deceafed having the
Character of a very ill Liver, moft People who heard
the Story, were apt to imagine this terrible Apparition came to attend his laft Moments.

A mighty Buftle they alfo make of an Apparition, which they fay, haunts Caftle *Ruſſin*, in th
Form of a Woman, who was fome Years fince executed for the Murder of her Child. I have heard
not only Perfons, who have been confined there for
Debt, but alfo the Soldiers of the Garrifon affirm
they have feen it various Times: but what I took
moft notice of, was the Report of a Gentleman
of whofe good Underftanding, as well as Veracity,
I have a very great Opinion. He told me, that
happening to be abroad late one Night, and catch-
ed in an exceffive Storm of Wind, and Rain, he
faw a Woman ftand before the Caftle Gate, which
being not the leaft Shelter, it fomething furpriz'd
him, that any body, much lefs one of that Sex
fhould not rather run to fome little Porch, or Shed
of which there are feveral in *Caftle Town*, than
chufe to ftand ftill expofed and alone, to fuch
dreadful Tempeft. His Curiofity exciting him to
draw nearer, that he might difcover who it was
that feemed fo little to regard the Fury of the
Elements, he perceived fhe retreated on his Approach, and at laft, he thought, went into the
Caftle, tho' the Gates were fhut. this obliging
him to think he had feen a Spirit, fent him home
very much terrified; but the next Day, relating
his Adventure to fome People who lived in the
Caftle, and defcribing, as near as he could, the
Garb and Stature of the Apparition, they told him
it was that of the Woman abovementioned, who

...ad been frequently feen, by the Soldiers on guard
...o pafs in and out of the Gates, as well as to walk
...hro' the Rooms, tho' there was no vifible Means
...o enter.

Tho' fo familiar to the Eye, no Perfon has yet,
...owever, had the Courage to fpeak to it, and, as
...hey fay, a Spirit has no Power to reveal its Mind
...ithout being conjured to do fo in a proper Man-
...er, the Reafon of its being permitted to wander
...s unknown.

Another Story of the like Nature, I have heard
...ncerning an Apparition, which has frequently
...een feen on a wild Common near *Kirk Jarmyn*
...ountains, which, they fay, affumes the Shape of
...Wolf, and fills the Air with moft terrible How-
...ngs.

But having run on fo far in the Account of fu-
...rnatural Appearances, I cannot forget what was
...ld me by an *Englifh* Gentleman and my particu-
...r Friend. He was about paffing over *Duglas*
...idge before it was broken down, but the Tide
...ing high, he was obliged to take the River; ha-
...ng an excellent Horfe under him, and one ac-
...ftomed to fwim. As he was in the middle of
...he heard, or imagined he heard, the fineft
...mphony, I will not fay in the World, for no-
...ng human ever came up to it. The Horfe was
...lefs fenfible of the Harmony than himfelf, and
...pt in an immoveable Pofture all the Time it
...ed, which, he faid, could not be lefs than three
...arters of an Hour, according to the moft exact
...lculation he could make, when he arrived at the
...d of his little Journey, and found how long he
...had been coming.

He, who before laugh'd at all the Stories told of

E

Fairies,

Fanies, now became a Convert, and believed a[...]
much as ever a *Manks* Man of them all.

As to Circles in the Grafs, and the Impreffio[...]
of fmall Feet among the Snow, I cannot deny bu[...]
I have feen them frequently, and once thought I[...]
heard a Whiftle, as tho' in my Ear, when no bod[...]
that could make it was near me.

For my Part I fhall not pretend to determine [...]
fuch Appearances have any Reality, or are on[...]
the Effect of the Imagination, but as I had mu[...]
rather give Credit to them, than be convinced b[...]
ocular Demonftration, I fhall leave the Point to b[...]
difcuffed by thofe who have made it more th[...]
Study, and only fay, that whatever Belief we ong[...]
to give to fome Accounts of this kind, there are [...]
thers, and thofe much more numerous, which m[...]
fit only to be laughed at, it not being at all co[...]
fonant to Reafon, or the Idea Religion gives us[...]
the fallen Angels, to fuppofe Spirits fo eminent[...]
Wifdom and Knowledge, as to be exceeded [...]
nothing but their Creator, fhould vifit the Ea[...]
for fuch trifling Purpofes as to throw Bottles a[...]
Glaffes about a Room, and a thoufand other as[...]
diculous Gambols mentioned in thofe volumi[...]
Treatifes of Apparitions.

The Natives of this Ifland tell you alfo, that [...]
fore any Perfon dies, the Proceffion of the Fune[...]
is acted by a fort of Beings, which for that [...]
render themfelves vifible. I know feveral t[...]
have offered to make Oath, that as they h[...]
been paffing the Road, one of thefe Funerals [...]
come behind them, and even laid the Bier on th[...]
fhoulders, as tho' to affift the Bearers. One [...]
fon, who affured me he had been ferved fo, t[...]
me, that the Flefh of his Shoulder had been [...]

m[...]

uch bruifed, and was black for many Weeks after.
There are few or none of them who pretend
t to have feen or heard thefe imaginary Obfe-
...es, (for I muft not omit that they fing Pfalms
the fame Manner as thofe do who accompany
e Corps of a dead Friend) which fo little differ
m real ones, that they are not to be known 'till
th Coffin and Mourners are feen to vanifh at the
urch-Doors. Thefe they take to be a fort of
endly Demons, and their Bufinefs, they fay, is to
n People of what is to befall them : according-
they give Notice of any Strangers Approach, by
ftamping of Horfes at the Gate of the Houfe
e they are to arrive. As difficult as I found
bring myfelf to give any Faith to this, I have
ofrently been very much furprized, when on vi-
a Friend, I have found the Table ready
and every thing in order to receive me, and
by the Perfon to whom I went, that he
edge of my coming or fome other Gueft,
good-natured Intelligencers. Nay, when
to be abfent fome time from home, my
have affured me they were informed
Means of my Return, and expected me
when I came, tho' perhaps it was fome
before I hoped it myfelf at my going abroad.
is Fact, I am pofitively convinced by many
but how or wherefore it fhould be fo, has
ently given me much matter of Reflection,
left me in the fame Uncertainty as before.
therefore, will I quit the Subject, and pro-
to Things much eafier to be accounted for
Having been fo copious in my Defcription of
e Spiritual Power, it will be expected I fhould
fomething of the Temporal Jurifdiction, which

is perpetually in Oppofition with the other, and is arbitrary but in two Things, *viz* That in the Cattle-Markets no Perfon, be he of ever fo great Condition, is permitted to cheapen or bid Money for any Beaft till the Lord's Steward has had the Refufal of it ; and that if any Man or Maid-Servant be efteemed extraordinary in their Way, either he the Governor, or the two Deempfters have the Power to oblige fuch a Servant to live with them for the Space of a Year, and receive no more than fix Shillings for their Service during the faid Time. This they call *Yarding*, and the Ceremony of it is performed in the following Manner : An Officer appointed for that Purpofe, caled a *Sumner*, lays a Straw over his, or her Shoulder, and fays, *By virtue of this you are* Yarded *for the Service of the* Lord *of* Man *in the Houfe of his Steward, Governor, or Deempfter*, which-ever of them it is that has given this Commiffion. But this is a Law of no Force in *Bifhop*'s Lands ; for which Reafon, all Servants who have any Apprehenfions of being *Yarded*, hire themfelves, if poffibly they can, to thofe who rent the abovefaid Lands ; or failing in that, as foon as they perceive an Officer coming near them, run to that Afylum, on which, when they have fet their Feet, they are fafe for that Time.

In all Things elfe the People are treated with the utmoft Lenity by the Government. The Officers and the Soldiery, who receive their Commiffions and Pay from the *Lord of Man*, are extremely courteous and civil, rather endeavouring to do all the good Offices they can, than in the leaft exerting any Authority. 'Tis to their Compaffion alone, that the poor Criminals fentenced by the Spiritual Court to that loathfome Dungeon under

er the Chapel at *Peel*, are not really confined
ere, but have the Liberty of the Castle. In fine,
ey are not only the best-bred, and most con-
sible Men in the Island, but likewise, generally
eaking, the least vicious, in spite of the little
egard they pay to the Ecclesiastical Jurisdiction.
As to their Law-Suits, they are neither expen-
e nor tedious, but that draws on a Misfortune as
d, if not worse Consequence than either of the
hers; which is, that the Over-cheapness renders
em frequent. When a Person has a mind to
mmence a Suit against his Neighbour for Debt,
has no more to do than to take out a Token,
ich is a Piece of Slate marked with the Gover-
's Name on it; and it is the same thing with an
rest in *England* the Price of these Tokens is
more than two Pence, and every Man being al-
ed to plead his own Cause, there is no Occa-
n for Counsellors, Attorneys, or Sollicitors.
e Ignorance, however, of the People, and their
apacity of Speaking for themselves in publick,
e given an Opportunity to some Men to set
for a kind of Lawyers, who take Fees, and argue
both Sides, as in the Courts of Justice elsewhere.
Their *Sheeding* Courts, the same with our
ms, are held but twice a Year, but then they
e a Court of Chancery, wherein the Governor
ole Judge, which, if there be Occasion, he may
d once every Week; and this gives so easy and
dy a Dispatch to all Differences, that there is
e to do at their Grand Assizes.
know nothing in their Statutes nor Punish-
ts particular, but this, which is, that if any
son be convicted of uttering a scandalous Re-
t, and cannot make good the Assertion, instead

of

of being fined or imprifoned, they are fentenced
to ftand in the Market-Place, on a fort of a Scaf
fold erected for that purpofe, with their Tongue
in a Noofe made of Leather, which they call
Bridle, and having been thus expofed to the View
of the People for fome time, on the taking off the
Machine, they are obliged to fay three Time
Tongue thou haft lyed. As whimfical as this Pu
nifhment may feem, I know not but, if introduc
in fome Places that I could name, it might put
greater Stop to Malice than any private Punifh
ment whatfoever ; becaufe, that tho' a Perfon w
has once fuffered this Shame, fhould be tempt
to commit the fame Crime a fecond Time,
would be to little purpofe, becaufe whatever
faid, would be fure to gain no Credit, after hav
been once recorded as a Lyar

And now having given as full a Defcription as
think can be expected from me of the Courts
Judicature, both Spiritual and Temporal, and
Punifhments decreed for Offenders in this Ifla
I fhall proceed to fay fomething of the Place i
which may be called, properly enough, a to
mountainous Defart, little Space being left
either Arable or Pafture, and nothing of a Wo
or Foreft in the whole Ifland. You may ride m
ny Miles and fee nothing but a Thorn-Tree, wh
is either fenced round, or fome other Precauti
taken, that fo great a Rarity fhall receive no P
judice Hedges they have none, but what
made with Clay ; but as they have great Quant
ty of Fern and Gofs, that ferves them to b
their Bread with inftead of Wood.

Yet, notwithftanding the prefent Scarcity
Timber, the Natives tell you, it was once a w
wo

oody Country ; infomuch that *Peel*, which was
iginally called *Pile-Caſtle*, took its Name from
ing at firſt no more than a huge Pile of Logs of
Wood, laid in ſo regular a Manner, as to form
ſtinct Apartments, and make it a Dwelling-
acc. But this is ſuppoſed to be before the
ood, and if we may give credit to Doctor *Bur-*
t's Theory of the Earth, that the World was
en one vaſt Continent, without any Diviſion of
e Lands by Seas or Rivers, 'tis eaſy to believe
at univerſal Flow of Waters might, on leaving
have thrown up the Earth in ſuch Mountains, and
ried the Trees beneath their monſtrous Weight.
'Tis certain that they have no Timber, but
hat they find in Bogs or Sloughs when they dig for
urf, and there is ſeldom any found in leſs than
or 15 Foot deep. In ſearching for it, they
metimes meet with greater Prizes : I myſelf ſaw
ery fine ſilver Crucifix, and many Pieces of old
oin, not only of Copper, but alſo of Gold and
ver. They were got into Hands which would
t be prevailed on to part with them, tho' they
ew neither the Age nor Meaning of them ;
herwiſe I would have ſent ſome to our Learned and
genious Antiquaries in *England*, who, perhaps,
ight by the Inſcriptions and Figures, have been
le to judge more truly of the former Govern-
nt, and Rulers of theſe People, than any of
ſe Traditions, which with them paſs for hiſto-
al Truths, but according to my Notion of Things
e no better than ſo many Fables. But as I could
t obtain the real Medals, I had the Privilege of
ing a Draught of ſome which I looked upon as
moſt curious of them.
The firſt of theſe were of Gold, the next Silver,

and

and all the others Brafs. But there were many, which I believe of greater Antiquity, but fo much impaired, that it was impoffible for the niceft Eye to take the Impreffion

Having mentioned thefe Curiofities, I muft not omit one, which, if true, was a much greater, and afforded more matter of Speculation to the Age it was found in, than any I have named. It was a Man perfect in all his Limbs and Features, and, what is yet more wonderful, in his Habit; tho by the make of it, he muft have lain under-ground upwards of an Hundred Years. This extraordi nary Difcovery, they fay, happened no longer ago than in theReign of King *Charles* the Firft · there are Perfons now living, who affured me their Fa thers faw it; and from hence they infer the Whole fomenefs of their Climate, fince the Earth of itfelf, only by being kept clofe, could preferve a human Body, unembowelled, unembalmed, from being corrupted, or even his Clothes from Rottenefs or Decay. But as greatly as I have heard this Story averred, I do not fet it down, either here, or in my own Mind, for undoubted Verity, but leave it to the Pleafure of my Reader to believe, as he thinks moft reafonable, concerning this, as well as the many other Prodigies of Nature, which no Man can give a full Account of this Ifland with out mentioning.

Among others, I know none which more juftly may be called fo, at leaft, of thofe which I am con vinced of the Truth of, than that of the *Water Bull.* An amphibious Creature, which takes its Name from the fo great Refemblance it has of that Beaft, that many of the People, having feen him in a Field, have not diftinguifhed him from one of

more natural Species : nor have the Cows any
tinct to avoid him, tho' if any happen to co-
ate with him, as they frequently do, the Creature they conceive, never has Life, nor any due
mation, but feems a rude Lump of Flesh and
n without Bones, and feldom brought forth with-
the Death of the Cow.

A Neighbour of mine who kept Cattle, had his
lds very much infefted with this Animal, by
ich he had loft feveral Cows : he, therefore,
ced a Man continually to watch, who bringing
Word that a ftrange Bull was among the Cows,
doubted not but it was the *Water Bull*, and
ing called a good Number of lufty Men to his
ftance, who were all armed with great Poles,
h-forks, and other Weapons proper to defend
mfelves, and be the Death of this dangerous
my , they went to the Place where they were
he was, and run all together at him : but he
too nimble for their Purfuit, and after tiring
over Mountains, and Rocks, and a great
ce of ftony Ground, he took a River, and a-
ded any further Chafe by diving down into it,
every now and then he would fhow his Head
e Water, as if to mock their Skill. I heard
Perfon, however, who being perplexed in this
ner, by one of thefe *Water-Bulls*, had more
ning, and taking a Gun with him, charged
a Brace of Bullets, fhot him as he was going
the River.

s to any Buildings of great Antiquity in this
d, there are now no Remains, after Caftle
n, and *Peel* Caftle, with the Churches about it,
he *Nunnery*, and the Fort at *Duglas*, each of
h I fhall defcribe in a particular manner.

That

That which is call'd the Nunnery, is situate
a good pleasant Part of the Country, about half
Mile from *Douglas*, and tho' now entirely out o
Repair, except one small Part of it, where th
present Major has his Residence, shows in its
Ruins that few Monasteries once exceeded it, e
ther in Largeness or fine Building There are
some of the Cloysters remaining, the Ceilings of whi
discover they were the Workmanship of the m
masterly Hands, nothing in the whole Create
but what is imitated in curious Carvings on t
The Pillars supporting the Arches are so thick, t
if that Edifice was erected with a Design to b fa
the Efforts of Time, nor could it, in more lo
toa i have elapsed since, the Coming of Chr
have been so greatly de ated, had it received
Injury but from Time. but in some of the dre
ful Revolutions this Island has sustained, it d
less has suffered much from the Outrage o
Soldiers, as may be gather'd by the Niches
standing in the Chapel (which has been one
finest in the World) and the Images or the
prosted in them being worn out, which see
ne happened out by Force.

Here has also been many curious Monum
the Inscriptions of which, tho' almost worn o
still retain enough to make the Reader know
Bodies of very great Persons have been e
here. There is plainly to be read on one of

Illustrissima Matilda filia --------

And a little lower, on the same Stone,

-------*Rex Mercia*--------

think there is great Probability that this was
 tilda, the Daughter of *Etkelbert*, one of the
 ngs of *England*, of the *Saxon* Race, since both
 w and *Hollingſhed*, agree that Princeſs died a
 cluſe : but as there is no Certainty, the Date
 ng entirely eraſed, I ſhall leave it to my Rea-
 to think of it according to his Pleaſure.
 But I am entirely of Opinion that *Cartefmunda*
 fair Nun of *Winchester*, who fled from the Vi-
 nce threatned her by King *John*, took Refuge
 this Monaſtery, and was here buried ; becauſe
 re is very plainly to be read,

Cartefmunda Virgo immaculata.

 eſe Words remain ſo legible, that I doubt not
 the whole Inſcription would have been ſo too
 not ſome barbarous and ſacrilegious Hands
 ke the Stone, leaving only one Corner of it,
 ich is ſupported by a Column, and on the Baſe
 Date is yet perfectly freſh.

Anno Domini 1230.

 e eral fine Figures, which ſeem deſigned by
 y of Hieroglyphic, have alſo been both the Or-
 nents and Explanation of theſe Tombs , but now
 emoliſhed, that one can only know by the Frag-
 nts they have been too excellent not to have
 ired a better Fate.
 n the midſt of a ſmall ſquare Court behind this
 apel is a ſort of a Pyramid of reddiſh Stones
 ented with Clay, on which formerly ſtood a
 s , and near it have been many fine Monu-
 nts, tho' not ſo magnificent as thoſe within the
 Chapel.

Chapel. From this Place you may go down by gradual Defcent to a Cell, built all of white Stor where ftood the Confeffional Chair; but this al lies now in Ruins: as does a great Gate, whic they fay, was once exceeding fine, and was nev opened but at the Initiation of a Nun, or the Dea of the Lady Abbefs Some Pieces of broken C lumns are ftill to be feen up and down the Groun but the greateft Part have been removed for oth Ufes. There are a vaft Number of Caverns u der ground, fome of which were built for Places Penance, others for Convenience. In fome the are narrow ftone Benches, which, by the excefs Dampnefs, are overgrown with Mofs, but all dark, and the very Entrance to them choaked with Weeds and Briars; fo little Veneration the prefent Inhabitants of this Ifland pay to t Antiquity, or the Memory of what was fo precio to their Forefathers, who were formerly fo religious, that when they went abroad, they on a Winding Sheet, to fhow they were not mindful of Death.

Tho' the Rivers in this Ifland afford great Pl ty of excellent Water, a Well belonging to t Nunnery is faid to have exceeded them all, has been, notwithftanding the many extraordin Properties afcribed to it, of late fuffer'd to dry

Here have alfo been many fpacious Gardens the Convenience and Pleafure of the Nuns, bu have heard a melancholy Account of the fe Tryal put on thofe who were fufpected to h been guilty of falfifying their Vow of Chaftity

Over a Place called the *How* of *Duglas*, wh the Extent of the Earl of *Derby*'s Dominion o Sea, there is a Rock vaftly high and fteep, about

M

...iddle of which is a Hollow not very different ...m the Fashion of an Elbow-Chair, and near the ...p, another much like the former. Whether ...se are made by Art or Nature, I cannot pretend ...determine, nor did I ever hear : but on the ...htest Accusation, the poor Nun was brought to ... Foot of this Rock, when the Sea was out, and ...ged to climb to the first Chair, where she sat ...the Tide had twice ebbed and flowed. Those ...had given a greater Cause for Suspicion, went ...to the second Chair, and sat the same space of ...ne. Those who endured this Trial, and de-...ded unhurt, were cleared of the Aspersion ...wn upon them But in my Opinion, the Num-... of the Fortunate could not be great, for be-...s the Danger of Climbing the ragged and steep ...k, (which now very few Men can do above ...y or forty Paces) the extreme Cold when you ...e to any Hieght, the Horror of being exposed ...e to all the Fury of the Elements, and the horrid ...pect of the Sea, roaring thro' a thousand Ca-...s, and foaming round you on every side, is e-...h to stagger the firmest Resolution and Cou-..., and without all question been the Destruc-...ot many of those unhappy Wretches.

...he Fort of *Duglas*, which commands the Bay, ...very ancient Building, but kept in good Re-

...They say that the great *Caratack*, Brother ...*onduca* Queen of *Britain*, concealed here his ...g Nephew from the Fury of the *Romans*, who ...in Pursuit of him, after having vanquished the ...en, and slain all her other Children. There ...rtainly a very strong and secret Apartment ...r ground in it, having no Passage to it ...a Hole, which is covered with a large

F   Stone;

Stone; and is called to this Day, *The Great Man's Chamber*.

The ancient Inhabitants of this Island seem to have taken a great Delight in subterranean Dwellings, for there is no one old Building in it, which has not at least an equal Number of Rooms under ground as above, and sometimes as much, if not more, richly ornamented with Carvings, and the Floors covered with Stone of different Colours which makes them appear as if inlaid, and are very beautiful to the Eye. This therefore I may be bold to say without injuring the Truth that however unpolite and savage those who now call themselves the Natives of *Man* may be, it had in it, in some Ages of the World, Persons of the most delicate and elegant Taste, and who in their Customs savoured of a Disposition rather inclined to the *Romantick* than the *Rustick*, as they are at this Time degenerated, even to the greatest degree that can be imagined.

My Reader will easily perceive how little I derogate from the Genteelness of their Manners when I shall tell him that Knives, Forks, or Spoons are Things of so little Use with them, that at the Houses which are counted the best, excepting the Governour's, the Bishop's, and the Lord Steward's you shall not find above three or four Knives at Table, where, perhaps, there are twenty Guests and as for Forks, they seem not to know what to do with them, for if a *Manks* Man, or Woman happens to be invited to an *English* Family, nothing can be more aukward than their attempting to make Use of them. They are admirably dextrous in dissecting a Fowl with their Fingers, and if the Operation happens to be more than ordinarily

ult, they take one Quarter in their Teeth, and
th both their Hands wrench the Limbs affunder.
his, I have feen done among very wealthy Peo-
e, and who would not deny themfelves thefe
nveniences, if they thought them of any Con-
uence. Nay, fo incorrigible are they in this
mour, that tho', whenever invited by the *Eng-*
or *Irifh,* they find thefe Utenfils at every Plare,
y wil not return the Complaifance at their
n Entertainments This Behaviour, at my firft
ning, put me in mind of *Æfop*'s Stoik, who in-
d the Fox to Dinner on Viands in long-neck-
Bottles; for I found good Provifion, but no
ans to come at it. But on my growing better
uainted with the Cuftom of the People, I ca-
d for the future a Knife, Fork, and Spoon in
Pocket.

n their Sports they retain fomething of the
adion Simplicity. Dancing, if I may call it
jumping and turning round at leaft, to the
dle and Bafe Viol, is their great Diverfion. In
mmer, they have it in the Fields, and in Win-
in the Barns The Month of *May,* is every
u ufhered in with a Ceremony which has fome-
ng in the Defign of it pretty enough, and, I be-
c, will not be tirefome to my Reader in the
onar.

n almoft all the great Parifhes they chufe from
g the Daughters of the moft wealthy Farmers
oung Maid, for the *Queen of May.* She is dreft
he gayeft and beft manner they can, and is at-
ded by about twenty others, who are called
us of Honour: fhe has alfo a young Man,
is her Captain, and has under his Com-
d a good Number of inferiour Officers. In

Op-

Oppofition to her, is the *Queen of Winter*, who,
a Man dreft in Woman's Clothes, with wooll
Hoods, Furr Tippets, and loaded with the warr
eft and heavieft Habits one upon another : in th
fame manner are thofe who reprefent her Atten
ants dreft, nor is fhe without a Captain and Trooph
her Defence. Both being equipt as proper Emble
of the Beauty of the Spring, and the Deformity of t
Winter, they fet forth from their refpective Qu
ters ; the one proceeded by Violins and Flutes,
other with the rough Mufick of the Tongs a
Cleavers Both Companies march till they m
on a Common, and then their Trains engage i
Mock Battle. If the *Queen of Winter*'s Forces, r
the better, fo far as to take the *Queen of* N
Prifoner, fhe is ranfomed for as much as pays
Expences of the Day.   After this Ceremony W
ter and her Company retire, and divert themfel
in a Barn, and the others remain on the Gr
where having danced a confiderable Time, t
conclude the Evening with a Feaft : the Quee
one Table with her Maids, the Captian with
Troop at another. There are feldom lefs than fi
or fixty Perfons at each Board, but, as I faid
fore, not more than three or fom Knives.

I muft not here omit that the firft Courfe a
Manks Feaft is always Broth, which is ferved
not in a Soop-Difh, but in wooden Piggins, e
Man his Mefs.   This they do not eat with Spo
but with Shells, which they call *Sligs*, very
our Muffel Shells, but much larger.

Chriftmas is ufhered in with a Form much
meaning, and infinitely more fatiguing.   On
24th of *December*, towards Evening, all the S
vants in general have a Holiday, they go no

all Night, but ramble about till the Bells ring
ll the Churches, which is at twelve a-Clock;
ers being over, they go to hunt the Wren,
after having found one of thefe poor Birds,
kill her, and lay her on a Bier with the ut-
Solemnity, bringing her to the Parifh-Church,
burying her with a whimfical kind of Solem-
finging Dirges over her in the *Manks* Lan-
e, which they call her Knell, after which
ftmas begins. There is not a Barn unoccupied
whole twelve Days, every Parifh hiring Fidlers
e publick Charge; and all the Youth, nay,
times People well advanced in Years making
ruple to be among thefe nocturnal Dancers.
his Time there never fails of fome Work be-
made for *Kirk Jarmyns*; fo many young Fel-
and Girls meeting in thefe Diverfions, Na-
too often prompts them to more clofe Cele-
ions of the Feftival, than thofe the Barn al-
; and many a Hedge has been Witnefs of
eatments, which Fear of Punifhment has after-
s made both forfwear at the Holy Altar in
tion. On Twelfth-Day the Fidler lays his
d in fome one of the WenchesLaps, and a third
n asks, who fuch a Maid, or fuch a Maid
marry, naming the Girls then prefent one af-
nother, to which he anfwers according to his
Whim, or agreeable to the Intimacies he has
notice of during this Time of Merriment.
hatever he fays is as abfolutely depended on
Oracle, and if he happens to couple two
e, who have an Averfion to each other, Tears
exation fucceed the Mirth This, they call,
g off the Fidler's Head, for, after this, he is
for the whole Year.

This

This Cuftom ftill continues in every Parifh, an
if any young Lad, or Lafs, was denied the Priu
lege of doing whatever came into their Heads
they would look on themfelves as infinitely injurec
This Time is indeed their Carnival, and they tak
and are allowed more Liberties, than, methink
is confonant with their Strictnefs in other Cafes.

The young Men here are great Shooters wit
Bows and Arrows. There are frequently Shoo
ing Matches, Parifh againft Parifh, and Wage
laid, which Side fhall have the better.

As for publick Shows, there are none, of ar
kind, exhibited in this Ifland, fo that the only
verfion of the better Sort of People, is Drink
which, indeed, they have an excellent Opport
nity to indulge ; the beft Wines, and Rum, ar
Brandy, being exceffively cheap, by reafon,
before obferved, of their paying no Cuftom for
and a Man may drink himfelf dead without mu
Expence to his Family.

They have no Fairs worth mentioning, ev
two, which are kept at *Kirk Patrick*, the one
Midfummer, and the other juft after *Michae*
To thefe the good Houfewives bring Thread a
Worfted of their own fpinning to be wove,
here alfo you may buy any fort of Linen or We
len Cloth the Country produces, but none
They fell no Trinkets at thefe Fairs, as at
Englifh ones, nor much Eatables, befides Bu
and Fowls, which Commodities are brought
Creels, a fort of Baskets made of Straw, which th
hang over their Horfes Necks, in the manner
Panniers, and will contain a great Quantity.

As to their Horfes, they are generally fleet,
fmall, and very hardy ; they wear no Shoes,

Corn, nor ever go into a Stable · but when
y come off a Journey, tho' the Weather be e-
fo bad, aie only turned loofe to graze before
r Doors, or in an adjoining Field.

Nor are their Owners of much lefs hardy Con-
:ions; the greateft part of them, of both
es, go barefoot, except on *Sundays*, or when
y are at Work in the Field, and have then on-
ma'l Pieces of Cows, or Horfes Hide, at the
om of their Feet, tyed on with Packthread,
ch they call *Carrans*. Their Food is common-
eri ings,and Potatoes,or Bread made of Potatoes;
notwithftanding the great Plenty of Salmon,Cod,
,Rabbits and Wild-fowl of all foits,the ordinary
ple either cannot, or will not afford themfelves
thing elfe They are, however,exceeding ftrong:
ve feen a little Woman tuck up her Petticoats,
carry a very lufty Man on her Back thro' the
r, and this they frequently do for a Piece of
ney, the Water being too deep for any but the
ives to pafs on Foot.

ngling and Shooting would be agreeable Di-
ons for Gentlemen here, were not the Air fo
mely cold and aguifh. 'Tis certain that there
t a Place in the known World, which affords
Fifh; I have feen Eels of fix Foot long, and
on of between four and five Foot, and wonder-
fweet and lufcious: nor is their Wild-Fowl
iot to any, efpecially the Woodcocks and
. They have alfo a kind, which I never
d of any where elfe; it is called a Puffen, and
a grey Colour, with a white Breaft, fome-
bigger than a tame Pigeon, and is good Food
eat frefh, only is too fat, and has fomething
fifhy Tafte, but is excellent when potted or
pickled,

pickled, and will laſt good for a whole Year. Theſe Birds are taken in a Place, called the *Calf of Man*, where they breed in great Quantities in the Holes of the Rocks. They both fly, and ſwim and dive in the Water like Ducks. The beſt Time for taking them, is in the latter End of *July*, and the Beginning of *Auguſt*.

Rabbits are in ſuch Plenty, eſpecially in the Months of *Auguſt* and *September*, that they may be bought for a Penny a piece, returning the Skins, which are the Perquiſite of the Lord of *Man*, and given to his Steward, who ſends them to *England* and *Ireland* by Perſons who come over every Year, on purpoſe to import them.

But as the Herring-Fiſhery is the moſt talked on abroad of any thing appertaining to this Iſland, I believe my Reader will be ſurprized that I have ſo long been ſilent on that Head: To comply therefore with his Expectation, and diſcharge, as well as in me lies, the Duty of an Hiſtorian, I ſhall give as perfect an Account of it as poſſible.

Tho' Herrings are taken all round this Iſland, yet the main Body of the Fiſher-Boats goes off from Port *Iron*, where the Fiſhermen are attended by a Clergyman, who joins with them in a ſolemn Form of Prayer, on the Sea ſide, to Almighty God, that he will be pleaſed to favour their Undertaking, and bleſs their Nets with Plenty. 'Tis the Opinion of many a learned Man, that there is no created Being on Earth, of which there is not a Similitude in the Sea, and the Creatures which I have ſometimes ſeen brought up with the Herrings, ſeem to confirm the Truth of this Conjecture. Nothing is more common, than for the Nets to be broke with the Weight of a Fiſh

ich they call a Sea-Ca'f, and, indeed, in the
ad, and all the upper Parts, differs nothing
n thofe we fee in the Field. But what does
m the moft damage, is the Dog-Fifh, which,
reafon of its Largenefs, tears the Nets, in fuch
anner, that they lofe the Herrings thro' the
es, and bring up no other Prize than that, of
ch, nothing but the Skin is of any Value. This
fo great a Grievance, that, formerly they put
ublick Prayers in all the Churches, that the
-Fifh might be taken from them; after which,
loft their whole Trade, for the Dog-Fifh was
n from them, but with it the Herrings alfo,
er of them coming near their Seas all that
on: on which they changed their Tone, and
ed with more Vehemence for the Return of
Dog-Fifh, than they did before for its De-
re. God was pleafed, they fay, to liften to
Complaint, and on their next going out, fent
both Herrings and Dog-Fifh, tho' not in
abundance as before. Whether this is Fact,
t, I will not pretend to fay; it, however,
s a good Moral, that we ought not to ex-
only Bleffings from the Hand of Heaven:
Evil muft be mingled with the Good, to the
we may be more dependant on Divine Provi-
, we fhould elfe be too apt to forget our Du-
nd perhaps, look on the Comforts we receive
Due, and the juft Reward of our Actions.
at my firft coming to the Ifland, I was ex-
ly follicitous in diving into the Manners and
our of a People, which feemed fo altogether
and different from all the other *Europeans* I
ver feen; I went to Port *Iron*, the firft Sea-
Fifhery, after my Arrival: where, falling

into

into difcourfe with fome of the Inhabitants, I he[re]
an Account given me, which, I think, would b[e]
doing something of Injuftice to the Publick t[o]
conceal.

I believe there are few People, who have n[ot]
heard of Mermaids and Mermen, tho' I never m[et]
with any, who looked on them as any thing mo[re]
than the chimerical Tritons and Amphitrites of t[he]
Poets, till accidentally falling in Company with [an]
old Manks Man, who had ufed the Sea man[y]
Years, he told me had frequently feen them, a[nd]
endeavoured to make me believe his Affurt[ion]
true, by a thoufand Oaths and Imprecations [on]
happening to mention this at Port Iron, they feem[-]
ed to wonder at my Incredulity, and gave me [the]
following Narration.

In the Time, faid they, that Oliver Crom[wel]
ufurped the Protectorfhip of England, few o[r no]
Ships reforted to this Ifland, and that Uninterru[p-]
tion and Solitude of the Sea, gave the Mermen a[nd]
Mermaids (who are Enemies to any Company b[ut]
thofe of their own Species) frequent Opportun[ities]
of vifiting the Shore, where, in moonlight Nig[hts]
they have been feen to fit, combing their He[ads]
and playing with each other, but as foon as t[hey]
perceived any body coming near them, they ju[mp]
ed into the Water, and were out of fight imme[di-]
ately. Some People, who lived near the C[oaft]
having obferved their Behaviour, fpread large N[ets]
made of fmall but very ftrong Cords, upon [the]
Ground, and watched at a convenient diftance [for]
their Approach. The Night they had laid t[his]
Snare, but one happened to come, who was [no]
fooner fet down, than thofe who held the Stri[ngs]
of the Net, drew them with a fudden Jirk, a[nd]

enclo[fed]

...osed their Prize beyond all Possibility of
...aping

...On opening their Net, and examining their
...tive, by the largness of her Breasts, and the
...uty of her Complexion, it was found to be a
...m ... , nothing continued my Author, could be
...e lovely, more exactly formed, in all Parts a-
...e the Waist, resembling a compleat young Wo-
...n, but below that, all Fish, with Fins, and a
...e spreading Tail. She was carried to a House,
...used very tenderly, nothing but Liberty being
...ied But tho' they set before her the best Pro-
...on the Place afforded, she would not be prevai-
...on to eat, or drink, neither could they get a
...rd from her, tho' they knew these Creatures
...e not without the Gift of Speech, having heard
...m talk to each other, when sitting regaling
...mselves on the Sea-side They kept her in this
...nner three Days, but perceiving she began to
...very ill with fasting, and fearing some Ca-
...ity would befal the Island if they should keep
...til she died, they agreed to let her return to
...Element she liked best, and the third Night
...open their Door, which, as soon as she beheld,
...raised herself from the Place where she was then
...g, and glided with incredible Swiftness, on her
..., to the Sea-side. They followed at a distance,
...faw her plunge into the Water, where she was
... by a great number of her own Species, one
...hom asked what she had observed among the
...ple of the Earth, nothing very wonderful,
...er'd she, but that they are so very ignorant,
... throw away the Water they boil their Eggs
...This Question, and her Reply, they told me, was
...nctly heard by those who stood on the Shore
...atch what passed.

As

As I had not yet attained a thorough Knowledge of the Superstition of these People, nor t
passionate Fondness for every thing that might
termed, *The Wonderful*, I was excessively surpri
ed at this Account, given with so serious an A
and so much, and solemnly averred for Truth,
perceived they were not a little disgusted at
Want of Faith, but to make a Convert of
they obliged me to listen to another, as odd
Adventure as the former, which they assured
was attested by a whole Ship's Crew, and happ
ed in the Memory of some then living.

There was about some forty or fifty Ye
since a Project set on foot, for searching for Tr
sures in the Sea , accordingly Vessels were got re
dy, and Machines made of Glass, and cased w
a thick tough Leather, to let the Person do
who was to dive for the (in my Opinion de
purchased) Wealth One of these Ships happ
ing to sail near the Isle of *Man*, and having he
that great Persons had formerly taken Refuge th
imagined there could not be a more likely Par
the Ocean to afford the Gain they were then
search of, than this They, therefore, let d
the Machine, and in it, the Person who had un
taken to go on this Expedition ; they let i. d
by a vast Length of Rope, but he still plucking
which was the Sign of those above to encrease
Quantity, they continued to do so, till they kn
he must be descended an infinite Number of
thoms. In fine, he gave the Signal so long,
at last, they found themselves out of Cord, t
whole Stock being too little for his capacious
quisition. A very skilful Mathematician being
board, said, that he knew by the Proportion of

which was let down, he muſt have deſcended
the Surface of the Waters more than twice
Number of Leagues that the Moon is compu-
o be diſtant from the Earth. But having, as I
no more Cord, they were obliged to turn the
el, which, by degrees, brought him up again;
eir opening the Machine, and taking him out,
peared very much troubled, that his Journey
o ſoon been at a Period, telling them, that
he have gone a little farther he ſhould have
ht Diſcoveries well worth the Search. It is
be ſuppoſed but every body was impatient to
formed of what kind they were; and being
thered about him on the main Deck, as ſoon
had recruited himſelf with a hearty Swill of
y, he began to relate in this manner.
ter, ſaid he, I had paſſed the Region of Fiſhes
ended into a pure Element, clear as the Air
ſereneſt and moſt uncloudedDay, thro' which,
aſſed, I ſaw the Bottom of the watry World,
with Coral, and a ſhining kind of Pebbles,
glittered like the Sun-Beams reflected on a
. I long'd to tread the delightful Paths, and
felt more exquiſite Delight, than when the
ine, I was encloſed in, grazed upon it. On
g thro' the little Windows of my Priſon, I
rge Streets and Squares on every ſide, orna-
d with huge Pyramids of Cryſtal, not infe-
Brightneſs to the fineſt Diamonds; and the
beautiful Building, not of Stone, nor Brick,
Mother of Pearl, and emboſſed in various
es, with Shells of all Colours. The Paſſage
led to one of theſe magnificent Apartments
open, I endeavoured, with my whole
gth, to move my Encloſure towards it, which

G   I

I did, tho' with great Difficulty, and very flow
At laft, however, I got Entrance into a very fp
cious Room, in the midft of which, ftood a lar
Amber Table, with feveral Chairs round of t
fame. The Floor of it was compofed of rou
Diamonds, Topaz's, Emeralds, Rubies, and Pea
Here I doubted not but to make my Voyage
profitable as it was pleafant, for could I h
brought with me but a few of thefe, they wo
have been of more Value than all we could lo
for in a thoufand Wrecks, but they were fo cle
ly wedg'd in, and fo ftrongly cemented by Time, th
they were not to be unfaften'd, I faw feveral Chai
Carcanets, and Rings, of all manner of precie
Stones, finely cut, and fet after our Manner; whi
I fuppofe, had been the Prize of the Winds
Waves: thefe were hanging loofely on the Ja
Walls, by Strings made of Rufhes, which I mo
eafily have taken down, but as I had edged m
within half a Foot reach of them, I was unfortu
ly drawn back, thro' your Want of Line. In
Return, I faw feveral comely *Mermen* and be
tiful *Mermaids*, the Inhabitants of this bl
Realm, fwiftly defcending towards it; but
feemed frighted at my Appearance, and glide
a Diftance from me, taking me, no doubt, for
monftrous and new-created Species.

Here, faid my Authors, he ended his Acc
but grew fo melancholy, and fo much enamo
of thofe Regions he had vifited, that he qu
all Relifh for earthly Pleafures, till continual
ings deprived him of his Life; having no H
ever defcending there again, all Defign of p
cuting the Diving Project being foon after la
fide.

With the fame Confidence the Truth of thefe
ratives were afferted, did I hear a Sailor pro-
that it was a common thing, when they were
at Sea, and too far from Shoar for the Voice
ny thing on Land to reach their Ears, for them
ear the Bleating of Sheep, the Barking of
, the Howling of Wolves, and the diftinct
of every Beaft the Land affords.

nothing is got, by contradicting a fictitious
ort, unlefs you can difprove it by more con-
ng Arguments than right Reafon can fuggeft,
ll Words, and, perhaps, worfe Ufage; I con-
d myfelf with laughing at them, within my-
and attempted not to lay before People, whom
d fuch Enemies to good Senfe, any Confider-
, how improbable, if not impoffible, it was,
ny body fhould give Credit to what they faid.
ould, however, have doubtlefs heard many
Accounts of the like Nature, if, by my fay-
tle in Anfwer to them, and a certain Air of
le, which they obferved in my Countenance,
hich, in fpite of my Endeavours to the con-
I was not able to refrain, they had not per-
that it was vain to attempt bringing me o-
their Side.

now having given as full an Account, as I
le, of the Wonders they relate of the fubter-
and fubterraqueous World, let me proceed
t is to be found by thofe who venture not
fh Expedients in the fearch of Curiofities.
rft of their Mountains.

y have many of a very great height, but
e three much fuperior to the others; the
called *Snafles*, from the Top of which, you
England, *Scotland*, and *Ireland*; the next,

Barool;

Barool; and the third, *Carrahan*. Under thes
they tell you, lie the Bodies of three Kings, fro
whose Names, the Mountains take their Denom.
nations, as they had their Rise from their Burial
for having in those Days no Notion of Architectu
or erecting Monuments, the only Way of per p
tuating the Memory of the Dead, was to throw
huge Pile of Earth over them : Every body, in p
sing, for a great number of Ages, thinking them
selves obliged to contribute towards the pic
Work, and throwing on a little, according to
Strength, or Time, they were Masters of, has rais
them to the stupendous Height they are now arriv
especially that of *Snafles*, under which, we ma' se
pose, either the greatest, most ancient, or most
loved Monarch lies. These rude *Mausoleums* ser
methinks, to shame the Pride of the modern Arc
tecture, being likely to continue, when those b
of Marble, with all their vain Infinity of Expe
and Art, will be crumbled into Dust, and di
into the Air, the Sport of every wanton Wind

The Bridges of any consequence in this Isl
are nine in Number, and called,

Castle-Town Bridge.

This is built of Stone, kept in good Repair
of a handsome Breadth, and so high, that a
with a Mast, may sail under it.

Ballasalli Bridge.

This is the oldest Bridge in the Island, and
also of Stone.

Kirk Braddon Bridge.

This is a strait Stone Bridge ; a fine River
under it, called the Dark River. Here is
Plenty of Fish, especially Eels.

D

Duglas Bridge.

This is lately broken down by the Rapidity of
[th]e River. A Woman, who was going over it,
[w]ith a Bottle of Brandy in her Hand, juft when the
[a]ccident happened, was faved by the Stiffnefs of
[he]r Hoop Petticoat, which kept her above Water.

Nunnery Bridge.

This Bridge has a Stone Foundation, but is board-
[e]d over and rail'd in, by reafon of the Turbulence
[of] the River, which fometimes threatens to over-
[flo]w it. Here they bring their Leather to foak.

Laxey Bridge.

This is the moft beautiful of any in the Ifland,
[ha]s handfome Seats to fit on, and is built over a
[fin]e River, which runs between two great Hills.

Peel Bridge.

Under this, is the moft famous River in the
[Ifl]and, it comes fram Kirk Jarmyn Mountains,
[an]d runs into the Sea, by the great Rock, on which
[fta]nds Peel Caftle.

The Millaroats his Mill Bridge.

This is a fmall Bridge, but built of Stone, and
[m]uch frequented.

Kirk Maroan Bridge.

A fine River, coming from Kirk Maroan Mount-
ins, runs under this Bridge to Kirk Santon.

There are, befides thefe, feveral fmall Bridges,
[bu]t not the twentieth Part fufficient for the Con-
[ve]nience of the Inhabitants ; yet, nothwithftanding
[a P]ropofal was made for building as many as were
[wa]nted, on every Houfekeeper's paying the Sum
[of] one Penny per Year for nine Years, it was not
[co]mplied with.

Having fpoken of the Manks Frugality, or ra-
[th]er Sordidnefs, in their Way of Eating, I muft

not

not omit making an Exception to this Rule, a
three feveral Times, which are their Wedding, a
their Chriftenings, and their Funerals.

As to the firft, twenty Pounds is a good Po
tion for a Mountaineer's Daughter, and they ar
fo exact in the Marriage-Bargain, that I hav
known many, who have called themfelves he
Lovers, break off for the fake of a Sow or a Pig be
ing refufed in the Articles. Yet, notwithftandi
this, a Stranger cannot be invited to one of the
nuptial Feafts, without believing himfelf in a La
of the utmoft Plenty, and Hofpitality. The Ma
is no fooner concluded, than befides the Banns
Matrimony being publickly asked in the Ch
three Sundays, notice is given to all the Frica
and Relations on both fides, tho' they live eve
far diftant. Not one of thefe, unlefs detained
Sicknefs, fail coming, and bring fomething to
wards the Feaft; the neareft of Kin, if they a
able, commonly contribute moft, fo that they ha
laft Quantities of Fowls of all forts I have fe
a Dozen of Capons in one Platter, and fix or ei
fat Geefe in another; Sheep and Hogs roa
whole, an Oxen divided but into Quarters.

They have Bride-Men, and Bride-Maids,
lead the young Couple, as in *England*, only w
this Difference, that the former have Ozier W
in their Hands, as an Emblem of Superior
they are preceeded by Mufick, who play all
while before them the Tune, *The Black and*
Grey, and no other is ever ufed at Weddi
When they arrive at the Church-Yard, they w
three times round the Church, before they e
it. The Ceremony being performed, they ret
home, and fit down to the Feaft, after which th

...ce in the *Manks* Fashion, and between that ... Drinking pass the Remainder of the Day.

...heir Christenings are not less expensive, the ... Country round are invited to them, and af-... having baptized the Child, which they always ... the Church, let them live ever so distant ... it, they return to the House, and spend the ... Day, and good Part of the Night in Feast-ing.

...hen a Person dies, several of his Acquaintance ... to sit up with him, which they call the ... The Clerk of the Parish is obliged to sing ...lm, in which all the Company join; and af-...at, they begin some Pastime to divert them-...s, having strong Beer and Tobacco allowed ... in great Plenty. This is a Custom borrow-...om the *Irish*, as are indeed many others, much ...hion with them.

...s to their Funerals, they give no Invitation, ...ery body, that had any Acquaintance with ...Deceased, comes either on Foot or Horseback. ...e seen sometimes at a *Manks* Burial, upwards ...hundred Horsemen, and twice the Number ...ot: all these are entertained at long Tables, ...d with all sorts of cold Provision, and Rum ...Brandy flies about at a lavish Rate. The Pro-...n of carrying the Corps to the Grave, is in ...Manner: When they come within a Quarter ...Mile of the Church, they are met by the Par-...who walks before them singing a Psalm, all ...Company joining with him. In every Church-...there is a Cross, round which, they go three ...es, before they enter the Church. But these ...e Funerals of the better Sort, for the Poor ...arried only on a Bier, with an old Blanket

round

round them, faftened together with a Skew

Having mentioned that there is no Chur
Yard without a Crofs, I cannot forbear taking
tice, that there is none which ferves not alfo fo
Common to the Parfon's Cattle; all his Hor
his Cows, and Sheep, grazing there perpetual
fo ftrangely is Religion and Rufticity mingled
gether in this Ifland !

Here, in juftice to thefe poor Peop'e, I muft
quaint my Reader, that however ftrange t
Tradition may feem of the Ifland being once
habited by Giants, my own Eyes were Witne
fomething which does not a little keep it in cc
tenance. As they were digging a new Vau
Kirk-Braddon Church-Yard, there was found
Leg-Bone of a Man very near four Foot in Le
from the Ancle to the Knee : nothing but ocular
monftration could have convinced me of the Tru
it, but the Natives feemed little to regard it, havn
they faid, frequently dug up Bones of the fame

They told me, that but a few Months b
my Arrival, there was found, under *Kirk-C*
Church-Yard, a human Head of that mon
Circumference, that a Bufhel would hardly
it ; and that nothing was more common, when
were digging, than to throw up Ribs and E
conformable to the Leg I had feen.

As it is a received Opinion, that the *Ant*
vians infinitely exceeded the Stature of M
fince the Flood, I can reconcile thefe Prodigi
otherwife to Reafon, than by judging them
the Remains of thofe who lived in the firft
of the World ; and that by a Virtue peculi
this Earth, have been preferved thus long
rifhed ; as they feem to make evident in the

...le before recited, of the Man whose very Flesh
...Clothes remain'd uncorrupted for the space of
...e than an hundred Years.

...heir Markets are kept on *Saturdays*, but there
...ttle Butcher's Meat to be bought by the single
...t, most of the Housekeepers, who do not bring
...Cattle themselves, join three, or four, or more of
...m together, according as their Families are in
...eness, and buy a Carcass; but as I before ob-
...ved, they are Persons of Consideration who eat
...at all, the Natives in general, both Rich and
...r, and many of the *Irish* who inhabit in the
...d, living almost wholly on Herrings and Po-
...es; the former of which, are pickled up in the
...son, and last the whole Year.

...his Island, therefore may be said to fit all Con-
...ons, and all Dispositions, the Poor and the Par-
...nious may live as cheap, and as miserable as
...wish; and People, who have full Pockets and
...ant Tastes, need want nothing to indulge the
...ury of the most *Epicurean* Appetite.

...or does the Eye want its Entertainment too;
...there are no Plays nor magnificent Sights to
...e it, here is every Charm that Nature can be-
...Rocks, Vales, Mountains, Rivers, Gardens,
...ter'd promiscuously in the most beautiful, tho'
...Variety imaginable. The Groves indeed,
...which Lovers are said so much to delight them-
...es, they cannot boast of, having, as I said be-
..., no Trees; but then there are a thousand a-
...eable Shades from the Mountains, and every
...re, except in Towns, the most charming Soli-
...e imaginable.

...hey have also one very great Happiness here,
...ch is, the not being infested with Robbers:
here

here are neither Highwaymen, nor Housebreake[r]
and a Man may leave his Doors unbarr'd, or tra[v]
the Island round without the least Danger of lo[sing]
his Money or his Life.

Silence, Solitude, and Security, being the Fr[iend]
of Contemplation, I fancy, if some of our g[ood]
Poets would take a Trip hither sometimes, th[ey]
would find their Account in it, and confess the I[m-]
provements their Genius's would receive in p[assing]
a few Months in a Place so retired, and at the [same]
time, so romantick, would very well compensa[te]
a short Absence from those noisy Pleasures, wh[ich]
rather serve to distract than any way to inform [the]
Mind.

Nor will any one deny there can be a Place m[ore]
proper for a Hermit, because here are no Tem[p-]
tations to allure him from his Cell, but he m[ay]
pass his Nights and Days entirely uninterrupte[d]
and as there are still many of those pious Men [in]
the World, it must be thro' Ignorance of this [Isl-]
and, that none of them made choice of it at p[re-]
sent · I say at present, because I have been she[wn]
a hole on the side of a Rock near Knk-Ma[n]
Mountains, which, they say, was formerly [the]
Habitation of one who had retired from the C[on-]
verse of Mankind, and devoted himself intirely [to]
Prayer and Meditation

What seems to prove this Conjecture is not wi[th-]
out foundation, is, that there is still to be seen [a]
Hollow, cut out on the side of a Rock with a rou[nd]
Stone at one End in the shape of a Pillow, wh[ich]
renders it highly probable to have been the h[umble]
Lodging of one of those holy Persons who h[ad]
forgone all the Gaieties and Pleasures of Life, [and]
chose to mortify the Body for the sake of the S[oul]

E[very]

...very thing, indeed, conſpires to prove that ...gion was once in very great Splendor in this ...d, but there are now little Remains of it, ex- ...in that blind Obedience paid to the Clergy, ...ich I have already fully treated, and the im- ...t Faith they give to every thing delivered from ...an in ſacred Orders. Among the many Im- ...ions put upon their Credulity, perhaps the ...wing Narrative may be an Inſtance.

... a wild and barren Field between *Balliſletcher* ...*Labnclegere*, there was a large Stone Croſs, ...n the many Changes and Revolutions which ...happened in this Iſland, has been broke down, ...part of it is loſt, but there ſtill remains the ...s Part. This has ſeveral times been attemp- ...o be removed by Perſons who pretended a ...n to whatever was on that Ground, and want- ...is piece of Stone: but all their Endeavours ...been unſucceſsful, nor could the ſtrongeſt ...n of Horſes be able to remove it, tho' Irons ...clapt about it for that Purpoſe. One Day, ...Tradition, a great Number of People being ...ted about it, contriving new Methods for the ...g it away, a very venerable old Man appear- ...nong the Crowd, and ſeeing a Boy of about ...ſeven Years of Age, he bad him put his ...d to the Stone, which the Child doing, it im- ...ately turned under his Touch, and under it ...ound a Sheet of Paper, on which were writ- ...heſe Words, *Fear God, obey the Prieſthood,* ...*o by your Neighbour as you would have him* ...*you.* Every body preſent was in the utmoſt ...ze, eſpecially, when looking for the old Man, ...der to aſk him ſome Queſtions concerning the ...ulous Removal of the Stone, he was not to

be

be found, tho' it was not a Minute that they
taken their Eyes off him, and there was ne
House nor Hut in a great distance, where he c
possibly have conceal'd himself. The Paper
however, carefully preserved, and carried to
Vicar, who wrote Copies of it, and dispersed t
over the Island   They tell you, that they ar
such wonderful Virtue to whoever wears them,
on whatever Business they go, they are certa
Success. They also defend from Witchcraft,
Tongues and all Efforts of the Devil or his Ag
and that a Woman wearing one of them in
Bosom, while she is pregnant, shall by no Acc
whatever, lose the Fruit of her Womb.

In a Creek, between two high Rocks, whi
verlook the Sea on this side of the Island, the
you also, that *Mermen* and *Mermaids* have
frequently seen. Many surprising Stories of
amphibious Creatures have I been told he
well as at Port *Leon*; but the strangest of all, is

A very beautiful *Mermaid*, say they, beca
much enamour'd of a Young Man who used to
his Sheep on these Rocks, that she would fred
ly come and sit down by him, bring him Pie
Coral, fine Pearls, and what were yet grea
riosities, and of infinitely more Value, had
fallen into the hands of a Person who knew
worth, Shells of various Forms and Figure
so glorious in their Colour, and Shine, the
even dazzled the Eye that looked upon them
Presents were accompanied with Smiles, Patt
the Cheek, and all the Marks of a most since
tender Passion, but one day throwing her
more than ordinarily eager about him, he b
be frighted, that she had a Design to draw h

Sea, and ſtruggled till he diſengaged him-
nd then ran a good many Paces from her ;
Behaviour ſhe reſented ſo highly, it ſeems,
e took up a Stone, and after throwing it at
ded into her more proper Element, and was
ſeen on Land again. But the poor Youth,
t ſlightly hit with the Stone, felt from that
nt ſo exceſſive a Pain in his Bowels, that the
as never out of his Mouth for ſeven Days,
End of which he died.

r is there any Neceſſity for one who is leſs in
thSolitude, to paſs his Time wholly in it. Rude
age as I have deſcribed the Cuſtoms and
rs of this People to be, there are yet ſome
ions to that general Rule ; inſomuch that a
always brought up in high Life, may find
nions polite and well qualified enough for
nverſation even among the Natives ; but
the chief Towns are ſeldom without ſome
, either *Engliſh*, *Iriſh*, or *Scots*, tho' the
number are of the two latter, 'tis eaſy to
agreeable Converſation is not impoſſible to
d.

ry great Enemy to having any good Fellow-
th one another, is the Belief the Natives
eſs'd of, and endeavour to inſpire into every
e, that there is not a Creek or Cranny in
nd, but what is haunted, either with Fairies
ts. A Perſon is thought very fool-hardy,
any Buſineſs carries him to the North-ſide,
s to ſtay out after the Cloſe of Day They
a Temerity has been fatal to many ; and
it, tell you a long Story of a Man, who
ng with his Neighbour, they went out to-
oward the Sea-Side to decide the Matter

with

with their Swords. In the Combat, the one ha[p]
pened to run the other into the Belly, with wh[ich]
Wound he fell, and the Conqueror was abou[t to]
return home, when his Wife coming to the P[lace]
and hearing what had befallen, ran to the poor M[an]
and to prevent his living long enough to relate w[ith]
whom he had fought, tore open the Wound [her]
Husband had made, and plucked out his Bow[els.]
This Murder, they say, was never difcovered [till]
the Author of it, confeffed it in the Agonie[s of]
Death: but the troubled Spirit of the unreven[ged]
continues to hover about the Place till this D[ay.]
When any Paffenger comes near his Walk, he c[ries]
out, *Who is there?* And if the Perfon fo called
makes any Anfwer, he is fure not to out-live t[hree]
Days.

Another Story on the oppofite Side of the If[land]
paffes not lefs current than this. The difturbed S[pir]
it of a Perfon fhipwreck'd on a Rock adjacen[t to]
this Coaft, wanders about it ftill, and fometi[mes]
make fo terrible a Yelling, that it is heard at an [in]
credible Diftance. They tell you that the Ho[ufes]
even fhake with it, and, that not only Mank[ind,]
but all the brute Creation within Hearing tre[mble]
at the Sound. But what ferves moft to encreaf[e the]
Shock, is, that whenever it makes this extraord[inary]
Noife, it is a fure Prediction of an approach[ing]
Storm; nor does it ever happen, fay they, [but]
fome Ship or other fplits, and its Crew are thr[own]
up by the Waves. At other Times the Spirit [cries]
out only, *Hoa! Hoa! Hoa!* with a Voice l[ouder,]
if any thing, louder than a human one.

About a League and a half from *Barool*, the[re is]
a Ho'e in the Earth, juft at the foot of a Moun[tain]
which they call the *Devil's Den*. They tel[l]

, in the Days of Enchantment, Perfons were
e confined by the Magicians ; and that it now
ains a very great Prince, who never knew
th, but has for the fpace of 600 Years been
d by Magic Spells , but in what Manner he
in what Form, none had ever Courage e-
h to explore. They add, that if you carry a
e, a Dog, or any other Animal to the Mouth
is Hole, its Hair will ftand an end, its Eyes
, and a damp Sweat cover its whole Body.
ge Noifes they alfo pretend have been heard
ue from this Place and I knew a Man once,
poffitively averr'd that his great Grandfather
huge Dragon, with a Tail and Wings that
ned all the Element, and the Eyes that feem-
vo Globes of Fire, defcend fwittly into it, and
that, heard moft terrible Shrieks and Groans
within.

hat gave rife to this Story, I imagine was, that
Cavern being pretty deep, and perhaps divid-
to feveral Partitions, the Winds having found
ance into the Cavities, occafion that rumbling,
ometimes whiftling Sounds, which the Super-
n of the Natives interpret for Groans, Shrieks,
whatever elfe their own wild Ideas happen to
it.

rmerly their current Money was Leather,
every Man of Subftance was entitled to
: not exceeding a certain Quantity limited
Law then in Force · this had no other Im-
n than the Maker's Name, and Date of the
But the *Manks* Money now current, are
and Halfpence, of a bafe mixed Metal, the
effion and Infcription are the fame on both,
n one Side, three Legs, commonly called the

H 2   th ee

three Legs of *Man*, the Infcription on that fi
is *Quocunque gefferis ftabit*, which the Natives to
lifhly apply to the Pofture of the Feet, being op
fite to each Word, but the true Meaning to
feems to be, *Carry it where you will, it won't*
or pafs On the other fide the Impreffion is a Ch
of Maintenance, with an Eagle and Child, the E
of *Derby*'s Creft; the Motto, *Sans changer*, wh
Motto the *Manks* Men would tranfer from
original Meaning, which was to exprefs the unbr
ken Loyalty of the Houfe of *Stanley*, to imply th
own Stedfaftnefs but if it is to be taken in th
latter Senfe, I fhall rather think, it only impor
the intrinfick Worthleffnefs of their Coin, for wh
there is no Change to be got.

Silver and Gold are Metals they had little a
quaintance with, till the Troubles of *England*
the Reign of *Charles* the Firft, at which T
feveral Perfons taking Shelter in this Ifland, br
ing over great Quantities, made it more fam
to them. But to this Day the Natives trade l
in either of them.

There was, however, one Perfon who difcove
fo great a Regard for the purer Metals, that he
ried a great Number of *Spanifh* Pieces of E
and Moidores, in a Hole in the Earth near the Ca
which, about fome forty Years fince were foun
Workmen who were digging to enlarge the Ea
Derby's Wine Vaults, but not knowing what
make of them, by reafon they had loft their Co
carried them to the Overfeer of the Works, wh
hear, was not quite fo ignorant of their Wort

At the fame time, they tell you was alfo ro
about 16 Yards deep from the Surface, a pa
Shoes made of Brafs, but of fuch a monft
Le

th and Bigneſs, that they would infinitely have
itted the Feet of the Giants ſet up in *Guild-*
in *London*. and this, among other Things,
s to prove the vaſt Stature of the *Antedilu-*
, for they will have it that this Iſland was in-
ed before the Flood, as I have already re-
ed.

because when I ſet myſelf down to write the
ry and Deſcription of this Iſland, I reſolved
e a much fuller one than has yet been pub-
, I muſt not omit any Particular, tho' never
gnificant in itſelf, which bears any weight
hem. I ſhall therefore preſent my Reader
wo or three Inſtances more of their Credu-
o the end he may be as perfectly acquainted
Native of the Iſle of *Man*, as if he had lived
them as long as I have done.

he Days of Enchantment, ſay they, a certain
Magician had by his Art raiſed for himſelf
oſt magnificent Palace that ever Eye beheld;
ne who, either out of Curioſity, or a Deſire
g entertain'd there, went to it, but was
iately converted into Stone, or at leaſt had
ppearance of it. ſo implacable an Enemy
e wicked Maſter of it to all his own Species,
ſerved only by infernal Spirits. He became
th ſo much the Terror of the whole Iſland,
Perſon would venture to live, or paſs with-
ral Leagues of his Habitation, ſo that all
e of the Country was in a manner deſolate,
great Loſs and Detriment of the Place in
. This had continued for the ſpace of three
when an Accident, or rather the peculiar
on of Divine Providence was pleaſed in
o deliver them from the Terrors of ſo cruel
hbour.

A.

A poor Man whom one may juſtly term a [P]il-
grim, having nothing to ſubſiſt on but wha[t is]
procured by imploring the Charity of thoſe ab[le to]
afford him Succour, happening to travel on t[hat]
Side the Iſland, not knowing any thing of the [Fame]
of this Enchanter, and perceiving no Houſe in[ha]-
bited, nor any Cottage even where he might g[et]
Lodging, and it growing dark, he was in te[rrible]
Apprehenſions of being neceſſitated to take up [his]
Lodging on thoſe bleak Mountains I have alr[eady]
deſcribed, yet wandering on as long as Light p[er]-
mitted, in hopes of better Fortune, he, at [laſt]
came within ſight of this Palace, which fill[ed his]
Heart with much Joy. Coming near it, he be[held]
large Piazza's, which ſurrounded that magnifi[cent]
Building, and believing theſe might ſerve him [for]
a Reſting-place, without being troubleſome to [any]
of the Servants, whoſe churliſh Diſpoſition in ſ[ome]
Places did not always afford a ready Welcom[e to]
Strangers, he choſe rather to content himſelf [with]
reſting his wearied Limbs on the marble [Floor,]
than entreat a Reception into any of the B[ed-]
which perhaps might be denied. In a wo[rd, he]
ſat down on a Bench in one of thoſe Piazza's, [and]
finding himſelf hungry, took out of his Po[cket a]
Piece of Meat and Bread, which he had begg'[d at]
the laſt Town he had paſs'd thro'; he had al[ſo a]
little Salt, which by dipping his Meat in the [Salt]
he happened to ſpill ſome on the Floor, on w[hich]
he preſently heard the moſt terrible Groans to [iſſue]
from the Earth beneath, vaſt Winds ſeemed [to be]
let looſe from every Quarter of the Element,
the Face of Heaven was deformed with Lightn[ing,]
the moſt dreadful Thunder rattled over his He[ad,]
and in leſs than a Moment this fine Palace w[as]

oud and lofty Piazza's, Portico's, and Brazen
s, vanished into the Air, and he found him-
n the midst of a wide, defart, mountainous
, without the leaft Appearance of any thing
d formerly feen. Surprifed as he was, he
tly betook himfelf to his Prayers, nor remo-
om his Knees till Day began to break ; when,
hanking God for bringing him fafe thro' the
ers of the Night paft, he made hat fpeed he
to the next Village, and relating the Ad-
re juft as it was to the Inhabitants, they
not at firft give credit to what he faid, but
in great Numbers towards the Place where
lace of the Necromancer had ftood. they
onvinced, and join'd in Prayers and Thankf-
g for fo great a Deliverance.

was prefently concluded from what the Pil-
faid, that the Salt fpilt on the Ground had
oned this Diffolution of the Palace; and for that
n, Salt has ever fince been in fuch Eftimati-
long them, that no Perfon will go out on any
al Affair without taking fome in their Poc-
much lefs remove from one Houfe to another,
, put out a Child, or take one to nurfe,
ut Salt being mutually interchanged , nay,
a poor Creature be almoft famifhed in
reets, he will not accept any Food you will
im, unlefs you join Salt to the reft of your
olence. This is fo univerfal a thing among
that a Perfon cannot be three Days in this
without being a Witnefs of the Truth of it,
asking the meaning of fuch a Veneration
t, will be told this Story as I have related
ich, fhould any one feem to doubt the Truth
would incur the Cenfure of the Inhabitants,

as

as a very prophane Perfon, and a Man who belie[v]ed neither God nor Devil.

A Perfon at his firft coming to this Ifland, wou[ld] be ftrangely amazed at the little Complaifa[nce] they pay to the weaker Sex. the Men riding [al]ways to Market on Horfeback with their Creel[s] each fide their Horfes full of Fowls, Butter, Egg[s,] or whatever they bring thither to difpofe of, a[nd] the Women following them on Foot over Ro[cky] Mountains, Bogs, Sloughs, and thro' very d[eep] Rivers, and all this without either Shoes or Stock[ings], carrying thefe fuperfluous Coverings, as th[ey] term them, under their Arms, till they come [to] the Market-Town; then they fit down all toge[ther] on the fide of a Hill, and put them on for Fafhi[on] fake, and let down their Peticoats alfo, which [be]fore were tucked up higher than their Knees, [for] the Convenience of wading thro' the Rivers, [and] to preferve them from the Mire of the Bogs [and] Sloughs.

But the Reafon for obliging the Females to [this] Hardfhip, is a very whimfical one, and fuch a o[ne] as I believe, cannot but afford fome Diverfio[n to] my curious Reader; I fhall, therefore, infert [it in] the manner it was told me by an old Native, [to] whom it had been handed down from many G[e]nerations as an undoubted Verity.

He told me, that a famous Enchantrefs fojou[rn]ing in this Ifland, but in what Year, he was [ig]norant, had, by her diabolical Arts, made her[felf] appear fo lovely in the Eyes of Men, that fhe e[n]fnared the Hearts of as many as beheld her. T[he] Paffion they had for her, fo took up all their Hea[rts] that they entirely neglected their ufual Occup[ati]ons; they neither plowed, nor fowed; neither b[uilt]

Hou[fes]

es, not repaired them ; their Gardens were all
rown with Weeds, and their once fertile
s were covered with Stones , their Cattle died
ant of Pasture, their Turf lay in the Bowels
Earth undug for , and every thing had the
arance of an utter Desolation : even Propa-
ceafed, for no Man could have the least In-
ion for any Woman but this universal Char-
who smiled on them, permitted them to fol-
d admire her, and gave every one leave to
himself would be at last the happy He
en she had thus allured the male Part of the
she pretended one Day to go a Progress
he Provinces, and being attended by all her
rs on foot, while she rode on a milk-white
y, in a kind of Triumph at the Head of them,
them into a deep River, which by her Art
ade them passable, and when they were all
a good way in it, she caused a sudden Wind
, which driving the Waters in such abun-
to one Place, swallowed up the poor Lovers
Number of 600, in their tumultuous Waves.
which, the Sorceress was seen by some Per-
who stood on the Shore, to convert herself
Bat, and fly thro' the Air till she was out
t, as did her Palfrey into a Sea-Hog or
se, and instantly plunged itself to the Bot-
f the Stream.
prevent any such like Accident for the fu-
hese wise People have ordained their Wo-
go on foot, and follow wheresoever their
the Men shall lead ; and this Custom is so
usly observed, as indeed all their Traditions
at if by chance a Woman is before, who-
es her, cries out immediately, *Tehi-Tegi!*

Tehi-

Tehi-Tegi! which, it seems, was the Name of [an]
Enchantrefs which occasioned this Law am[ong]
them.

But in my Opinion, there is little occa[sion]
this Day for putting it in Practice, for how m[uch]
soever the Natives of *Man* might formerly d[evote]
themselves to the Will and Pleasure of their [Mis-]
tresses, they now use them with so little Cerem[ony]
that I wonder how these poor Creatures can [re-]
taste any Felicity in Love, or indeed, can be br[ought]
to endure the Marriage-Yoke, where there [is so]
little to compensate for the Servilities it re[duces]
them to, in a Climate so uncourteous to the[m.]

They tell you also, that their Ifland was [very]
much larger than it is at present, but that a [Ma-]
gician, who had great Power over it, and com[mit-]
ted many wonderful and horrible things, a[nd be-]
ing oppofed by one who was a Friend to the [Ifl-]
and, at length, overcome by him, he, in re[venge]
raifed a furious Wind, not only in the A[ir, but]
alfo in the Bofom of the Earth, which rend[ing]
tore off feveral Pieces; which floating in th[e Sea]
in Procefs of time were converted into Stone [and]
become thofe Rocks, which are now fo dange[rous]
to Shipping. The fmaller Fragments, they['ll fay, are]
Sanus, which waving up and down, are at [fome]
times to be feen, and at others, fhift themfe[lves]
off the Coaft. They maintain that it was on[e]
of thefe, that the late King *William* had like [to]
have perifhed, and ftrengthen this Sugge[ftion by]
the Trial of the Pilot, who muft infallibly [have]
been hang'd, if on ftrict Examination of a[ll the]
Charts, there had been in any of them the [leaft]
mention made of any fuch Sands, but howeve[r it]
be, thefe floating Ruins have ever fince rema[in-]

om thence are called *King William's Sands.*
now, I believe, my Reader will be almost as
ued with reading this Description, as I am
riting it; and having nothing more to say,
can flatter myself will be either instructive or
ining to him, shall take my leave, wishing no
man, who has ever known the polite Plea-
f Life, may deserve so ill of Heaven, as to
en into this Banishment through Necessity;
think it will not be loss of Time to those
avel in search of the Wonders of Nature, to
Trip to it, since I believe there is no Place
er in the known World, abounds with more
e *Isle of Man.*

F I N I S.

CPSIA information can be obtained at www.ICGtesting.com
Printed in the USA
LVOW112150181112

307905LV00004B/204/P